Fundamentals of Credit

And

Credit Analysis

Corporate Credit Analysis

Arnold Ziegel
Mountain Mentors Associates

Table of Contents

Chapter 9 Managing Credit Risk - Risk Ratings and Portfolio Management

Preface

Arnold Ziegel formed Mountain Mentors Associates after his retirement from a corporate banking career of more than 30 years at Citibank. The lessons learned from his experience in dealing with entrepreneurs, multinational corporations, highly leveraged companies, financial institutions, and structured finance, led to the development and delivery of numerous senior level credit risk training programs for major global financial institutions from 2002 through the present.

This book was conceived and written as a result of the development of these courses and his experience as a corporate banker. It illustrates the fundamental issues of credit and credit analysis in a manner that tries to take away its mystery. The overriding theme of this book is that when an investor extends credit of any type, the goal is "to get your money back", and with a return that is commensurate with the risk.

The goal of credit analysis is not to make "yes or no" decisions about the extension of credit, but to identify the degree of risk associated with a particular obligor or a particular credit instrument. This is consistent with modern banking industry portfolio management and the rating systems of credit agencies. Once the "riskiness" of an obligor or credit instrument is established, it can be priced or structured to match the risk demands or investment criteria of the entity that is extending the credit.

A simple quote from Mr. J. P. Morgan is used often in this text - *"Lending is not based primarily on money or property. No sir, the first thing is character"*. This statement represents one of the conflicts in modern credit analysis – that of models for decision making versus traditional credit analysis. The 2008 financial crisis was rooted in the mortgage backed securities business. Sophisticated models were used by investors, banks, and rating agencies to judge the credit worthiness of billions (and maybe trillions) of dollars worth of residential mortgage loans that were packaged into securities and distributed to investors. The models indicated that these securities would have very low losses.

Of course, huge losses were incurred. Mr. Morgan had a good point. In this case is was both property and character. The properties that were the collateral for many of the mortgages had much less value than was anticipated. The valuation of the collateral was naïve and flawed. Many assumptions were made that the value of homes would rise without pause. Many mortgage loans were made that were at or even above the appraised value of a residence.

But character was a huge, perhaps larger, factor behind these losses. Many of the residential mortgage loans were made to individuals who knew that they did not have the income to make the required payments on the mortgages. Many of the mortgage brokers and lenders who made these loans also knew that many of the borrowers were not properly qualified. And, many of the bankers who securitized these loans also may have doubted the credit quality of some of the underlying mortgages. If bankers and rating agencies understood the extent of the fraud and lax standards in the fundamental loans backing the mortgage securities, or were willing to acknowledge it, the fiasco would not have occurred.

Thanks are due to Keith Waitt of Consultancy Matters, who encouraged and facilitated the development of these credit risk training programs; and Ronna Ziegel, Ph.D., who established the basis for the teaching philosophy and techniques.

Arnold Ziegel
Mountain Mentors Assocates
Stowe, Vermont
2014

Chapter 1

Introduction – The Goals and Nature of Credit Analysis

Credit analysis is an art, not a science. The goal of credit analysis is to make a judgment about an obligor's ability and willingness to pay back what it owes, when it is owed. Obligations could be a loan, bond, trade payable, or any kind of financial contract.

The fundamental question that a credit analyst needs to answer is: "what is the degree of risk that an obligor will have sufficient cash to pay back an obligation when it is due?" If the obligation is short term, and the obligor has a lot of liquidity, the answer is usually easy to determine.

If the time frame is longer, the answer to this question is not easy. The credit analyst must assess the factors that will impact an obligor's ability to pay in the future, including the willingness to pay. The basis for this assessment is the prediction of future cash flow, future liquidity, and capital structure.

In order to make a judgment about the degree to which cash will be able to fulfill an obligation in the future, the credit analyst must be able to project future cash flow, and make an assessment about the risks associated with that projection. Analysis of historical financial performance is usually the starting point for the estimates of future performance. Assessing the capital structure relative to the operating risks is a critical indicator of the degree of "financial" risk that the obligor is incurring. But, financial analysis must be supported by the logic of assessing business strategy and industry key success factors. Events don't' happen by themselves – assessing management capability is also critical to the forecasting process.

Judgments must be made about the forecasts of future performance relative to history, future capital structure, management capability, business strategy, competitors' performance and competitive pressure, and the macro-economic environment. If the future revenue generation of the obligor is risky, due to the nature of the business, the strategy, and environment (i.e., it has high operating risk), then the capital structure should be relatively conservative. If future revenue and cash flow seems to be stable with little risk, then the capital structure can have higher degrees of leverage and "financial risk".

Equity analysts try to estimate the value of a company.

Credit analysts try to establish the degree to which an obligor can fulfill the terms of its debt obligations – short term and long term

Both equity analysis and credit analysis require the use of significant judgment to assess future performance and future cash flow.

Estimates of future cash flow are the basis for all securities valuation – equity and debt.

The art of both equity and credit analysis rests upon the understanding of the many factors that can impact future cash flow, and making judgments about those factors. While the value of equity may be enhanced by the use of a lot of debt (leverage), this adds risk to the creditors of the obligor. At some point, high degrees of leverage can substantially increase the risk of bankruptcy. Finding the balance between operating risk (business risk) and financial risk (capital structure) is a key element of the role of the credit analyst.

A borrower / obligor rarely suggests that it will not be able to generate the cash necessary to repay an obligation when it is due! The job of the credit analyst is to use financial analysis, industry analysis, strategy analysis and management analysis to make a reasonable judgment about an obligor's ability to have the cash on hand to fulfill the terms if its obligation. That judgment takes the form of an assessment of the degree of risk associated with the ability to do so – the generation of cash from operations, and the nature of the capital structure.

In traditional bank credit training, the process of credit analysis is framed by three simple questions:

Who's the borrower?
What's the purpose of the loan (or other type of obligation)?
How and when will it be paid back?

The analysis to be done to answer these questions can be addressed in another traditional way, referred to as the four "C's" of credit – capacity, capital, condition and character (some consider another "C", collateral).

Capacity is the ability to generate enough cash to repay all obligations, when due. Assessing this is a primary goal of credit analysis.

Capital is required during periods of weak cash flow generation for a company to sustain itself. If there isn't sufficient cash flow from operations to meet obligations, then assets may have to be sold to produce cash.

Condition refers to the macro economic and competitive environment which will impact an obligor's future performance and its ability to generate cash.

Character is not only the willingness to repay an obligation, and live up to its terms, but also honesty relative to the risk of fraud. It might also refer to the competence of the obligor.

The challenge for the credit analyst is to move from these simplistic statements to a framework for reaching an answer to this question:

"What is the degree of risk that an obligor will be able to have a sufficient amount of cash to pay back the obligation when it is due?"

Of course, the degree of risk ranges from "zero risk" to "a lot of risk". The goal of credit analysis is to establish where an obligor, and specific obligations, fits into this range. In modern bank risk management, this is analogous to determining a "risk rating". It is also analogous to a public debt rating established by Moody's or Standard and Poor's.

Short term credit obligations are often "rolled over" or extended. But if the holder of the debt demands payment, this will come from a company's liquidity. Either from cash on hand, or the natural cash generated from the collection of accounts receivable or the liquidation of inventory.

Repayment of long term debt comes from cash on hand, cash flow generation or refinancing. But, refinancing of long term debt will occur only if the lender is confident that the borrower has the ability to generate cash flow to repay it, or the ability to sell large amounts of assets to repay.

Credit Risk and Cash Flow Volatility

The degree of risk associated with a company's cash flow is related to the volatility of its cash flow. High credit risk is often due to highly volatile cash flow. Low risk is a function of very low volatility of cash flow.

For example, think about the volatility of the rental income from an office building that is fully leased, in its entirety, to a highly rated corporation for a very long term, with that corporation paying all operating costs and maintenance and taxes. The risk of the cash flow from those rental payments is not related to the office building, but only the credit of the corporate tenant. The credit risk of a mortgage loan made to finance this building would have risk characteristics very similar to that of the long term corporate tenant. The cash flow volatility associated with that property would be very low, especially if the tenant is a low credit risk corporation. The risk would vary with the credit risk of the tenant.

On the other hand, the risk of a mortgage loan for the same building, but with no major long term tenant, might be very high. It would be real estate risk. To make a judgment about this, the credit analyst would have to do extensive research about current and historic rental rates, occupancy rates, the existence of competitive buildings and plans for new ones, and the macro-economic outlook for the demand for office space in the location. An appraisal would be obtained to establish an independent view of the building's value, but this should not be the only basis for establishing the degree of risk of the potential loan.

Highly risky (volatile) future cash flow doesn't mean that a particular loan or obligation has to be risky. A good lending officer or risk manager can structure a loan to remove some of the risk. For a general corporate loan, the analysis can focus on a "second way out". If the borrower can't generate sufficient cash to repay an obligation, it can hopefully raise cash in a second way – usually through the sale or liquidation of an asset. This can be a variety of assets available to the obligor, or a specific asset that might be identified and secured.

An obligation can be structured such that the risk of the specific obligation is actually lower than the overall risk of the obligor. Collateral (security) is used to accomplish this. Some very secure loans are made to bankrupt companies! Where this is done, the risk rating of the specific obligation could be much better than the risk rating of the bankrupt company. The probability of the secured obligation being repaid on time could be very high, due to the nature of the collateral. On the other hand, the ability to forecast the repayment of unsecured obligations to a bankrupt company would be very difficult.

The phrase "ring fencing" is often used in corporate finance for transactions that are structured to isolate the risk of a particular financing. It implies that cash flow associated with a particular project, or structure finance entity, will be dedicated entirely to the repayment of debt incurred by that entity. Project finance, dedicated financings for a road, mine, etc, are structured to ensure that all of the cash flow generated by the project can first be allocated to the repayment of the debt incurred by that project.

The credit crisis of late 2007 was a result of the flawed assessment of collateral used to reduce risk in structured finance entities. The "CMO's" (collateralized mortgage obligations) were secured by home mortgages in The United States. The credit quality of the individual obligors was relatively low (maybe very low), but each loan was secured by a residence. There seemed to be a very low risk that losses in a "pool" of mortgages (the CMO) would exceed a certain level. The crisis occurred because default rates turned out to be much higher than anticipated, the value of the collateral (the mortgages on homes) turned out to be less than the amount of the mortgage loans, and the actual losses in these pools of mortgages far exceeded what was forecast. The credit analysts for many of these CMO's did a poor job of forecasting cash flow of the individual borrower's, as well as the value of the underlying collateral. Many of the mortgage applications apparently were fraudulently underwritten.

Summary of the Introduction

The fundamental question of credit analysis is: "what is the degree of risk that an obligor will have sufficient cash to pay back an obligation on a timely basis?" The "art" of credit analysis is to understand how to convert historic financial and operating performance and financial condition into a judgment about an obligor's willingness and ability to repay an obligation in the future, and the degree of risk around that judgment. The traditional four "C's" of credit analysis still provide a valid, if simplistic, framework for this process – assessing Capital, Capacity, Conditions, and Character.

An appropriate capital structure is one that provides adequate returns to the equity investors, while not incurring so much debt that the risk of bankruptcy becomes very high. A good credit analyst will always be assessing the quality of an obligor's capital structure, and the degree of risk that it creates for the various suppliers of capital. A company's capital structure should be designed to match financial risk with the nature of its business risk. A company with very low business risk can safely assume a lot of balance sheet (financial) risk in the form of leverage (debt). A company with very high business risk will not survive for long if it also assumes a great deal of financial risk (leverage).

The remaining chapters of this course cover more specific aspects of credit analysis, including:

Fundamentals of financial analysis

Fundamentals of credit analysis – cash flow forecasting and debt capacity. Assessing financial position, capital structure adequacy and relative risk. Short term debt capacity. Long term debt capacity.

The goals and requirements of various suppliers of credit and capital to companies, including trade creditors, commercial banks, private investors, and institutional investors – expectations about risk and return

Credit facility structure and secured lending

Modern risk management in commercial banks and the concept and use of risk ratings in banks and by rating agencies

Chapter 2

Capital Structure and Debt Capacity

Balancing Operating / Business Risk and Financial Risk

A company's capital structure is comprised of a combination of debt and equity that is used to fund the assets on its balance sheet.

Example for the following discussion: XYZ Company

Assets

Short Term:	
Cash	100
----Accounts Receivable	20
Inventory	20
Pre-Paid expenses	5
Total Short Term (Current)	145
Property	200
Equipment	100
Investments	50
Total Long Term Assets	350
Total Assets	495

Liabilities

Current Liabilities	60
Long Term Debt	0
Equity	435

The "right" capital structure for any company is a function of the nature of the assets being funded, the volatility of the company's future cash flow, the availability of sources of capital, and the tolerance for risk by the owners and suppliers of capital.

A company can support a lot of debt if its cash flow is stable, and/or its assets are liquid. If the company's future cash flow is subject to a lot of risk (high volatility) and its assets are relatively illiquid, it might have difficulty paying interest and principle at some future point, depending upon the amount of its debt, and the terms of repayment. Debt capacity issues for companies are not very different from that of individuals! It all hinges on the future of cash flow – volatile or stable.

If a borrower's future cash flow is subject to a lot of risk, equity is the appropriate source of funding and will be the dominant part of the capital structure.

In order to boost their return on investment, equity owners have an incentive to use debt (leverage) to buy assets that will be used to produce revenue and profit. If the return on these assets is greater than the cost of debt, the benefit accrues to the owners of the company. While we expect owners to be prudent and not incur more debt than they can afford, sometimes they are overly aggressive, or just do not know how much debt can be safely incurred. It is the job of the credit analyst to answer this question – "what is the debt capacity of a company?"

Capital Structure and its Impact on Return on Equity (ROE)

Common Equity is the fundamental part of a company's capital structure. It is the funds that belong to the owners. It has no date at which it must be returned (maturity) and no legal obligation to pay dividends. It is contributed when a company is formed, and builds as a company generates, and retains, profits.

The goal of the owners of equity is to generate a good return on their investment (Return on Equity, ROE). If a company does not produce an ROE that is greater than its "cost of capital" then it is destroying value for the owners of its equity. They'd be better off taking their money and investing it elsewhere. Of course, this is not a short term decision, and most equity owners would look to the future, estimate/forecast future returns, and try to judge the present value of the future returns, using their cost of capital as the discount rate. Hopefully it's positive. Obviously this is highly subject to the evaluation of the risk associated with the forecast of future returns. If it's not positive, the investors should take their money and invest it elsewhere where they can get a positive, risk adjusted, return on capital.

Return on Equity is a function of three variables – profit margin, asset turnover, and leverage. This is a simple analytic model that can explain the basic business model of any company. ROE is produced by some combination of these three variables – high margins, high asset turnover, high leverage, or some combination of all three. Since high leverage is only sustainable in companies that are very stable with predictable revenue, most companies have to focus on profit margins and asset turnover to produce an adequate ROE.

In the case of XYZ Company (above), the equity is 435. If the owners expect a return on their capital of 10% after tax (which is a relatively modest expectation), the company must be able to figure out how to generate 43.5 after tax from a balance sheet with total assets of 495. Assuming a tax rate of 35%, this is pre-tax profit of about 67.

How does a company produce 67 of pre-tax operating profit with a balance sheet of 495? It has to figure out how to generate enough revenue from its assets, at a sufficient profit margin, and with a degree of leverage that doesn't risk putting itself into bankruptcy.

Using the XYZ company balance sheet, we can look at a few ways to produce the desired return on equity of 10%.

As shown above, a 10% return on 435 of equity is 43.5.

Return on equity = net profit / average equity

In this case ROE = 43.5 / 435 = 10%

Leverage is the ratio of total assets that are funded by equity. It also can be measured as the ratio of debt / equity, but for this example we'll stay with the ratio of total assets to equity. Leverage = assets / equity.

In this case, Leverage = 495 / 435 = 1.138   Total assets are equal to 1.138 times total equity. This would be considered to be very low leverage. This is the same as Equity is funding 88% of total assets (435/495).

If XYZ is in an industry that produces very low profit margins, such as retail grocery chains (supermarkets), the after tax profit margin would generally be about 2% (after tax). How much revenue is necessary to produce 43.5 of after tax profit at a 2% margin? It's 2175!

Or, 2175 X .02 = 43.5

If XYZ was in a business that had much higher profit margins, say 25%, it would only need revenue of 174 to produce its profit of 43.5.

Companies operate with different economic models, depending on the nature of their business and industry, the nature of their assets, the competitive situation and the economic environment.

If XYZ had revenue of 2175, a profit margin of 2% and Equity funding 88% of total assets, its ROE would be 10%.

This analytic model has been attributed to a Treasurer of the DuPont company, and is often referred to as the "DuPont" model. It is an algebraic equation that illustrates the relationship that ROE is a mathematical function of three variables – profit margin, asset productivity, and leverage.

Profit margin is equal to Profit / Revenue = 43.5 / 2175 = .02 = 2.0 %

Asset turnover is defined as Revenue / Assets = 2175 / 495 = 4.39 Every unit of assets produces 4.39 units of revenue in a given period of time. This represents a highly productive balance sheet!

Leverage is often defined as debt / equity. In this model we use total assets / equity, which is the proportion of assets that are funded by equity, as opposed to the proportion of assets that are funded by debt.

Leverage = assets / equity = 495 / 435 = 1.138

The DuPont model uses basic algebra to prove that a company's **RETURN ON EQUITY** (ROE), is absolutely a function of three key variables – **PROFIT MARGIN** (net profit / revenue), **ASSET TURNOVER** (revenue / assets), and **LEVERAGE** (assets / equity).

Net Profit / Equity = Net Profit / Revenue X Revenue / Assets X Assets / Equity

In the above formula, using basic algebra, "Assets" cancel out and "Revenue" cancels out, leaving Net Profit / Equity = Return on Equity!

In the case of XYZ, the leverage is 1.138 – assets of 495 and equity of 435. In order to produce an ROE of 10%, it must find some combination of asset turnover (revenue / assets) and profit margin (net profit / revenue), to achieve this.

XYZ company is actually modelled on a supermarket, with a low, but typical, profit margin of 2%. Using the DuPont formula, in order to produce an ROE of 10%, the asset turnover must be 4.394. In other words, the balance sheet of 495 must somehow produce total revenue of 2175!

ROE (10%) = leverage (1.138) X asset turnover (4.394) X profit margin (2%)

10%	=	1.138	X	4.394	X	.02
ROE	=	everage	X Asset Turnover		X Profit Margin	

If the XYZ company was in an industry where it was able to obtain a profit margin of 25%, not 2%, it would only need to produce revenue of 174 to produce the 43.5 of net profit necessary for a 10% return on equity.

```
10%    =    1.138    X   (174 / 495 = 0.352)   X    .25
ROE    = Leverage  X  Asset Turnover          X Profit Margin
```

Is it possible that one company can operate with a profit margin of 2% and another with 25%? What are the factors that might allow this or cause this? This is what the credit analyst must understand in order to judge whether or not a company's business model is reasonable, especially relative to its capital structure.

The factors that cause different industries to operate with different combinations of profit margin, asset turnover and leverage are a function of the nature of the business and competition. Supermarkets operate with very low margins for a variety of reasons. First, they are in a highly competitive industry. Competition severely restricts the ability to manage prices. Second, they sell merchandise that, by definition, has very high natural turnover. Things don't sit on the shelves very long in a well managed supermarket. Fixed assets (stores, fixtures, and equipment) represent a relatively small proportion of the total assets of a supermarket. Most of the assets will be in the form of inventory which should turn over very quickly.

The original idea for the discount department store (like Wal*Mart) is based on this concept. In order to obtain a certain Return on Equity, the owners created a lost cost environment and reduced prices, with the idea that they could sell a lot of merchandise with a given fixed cost. It worked! Low profit margin, but very high turnover, produced huge profits, even with little leverage.

A company with a very high profit margin will invariably possess a very significant competitive advantage. A software developer such as Microsoft might be an example. Most of its assets are equipment and facilities. Its revenue is the result of intellectual investment and the profit margins are a function of its very strong market position. Some have accused it of having almost a monopoly in certain of its products.

If a company finances its assets with all equity, its return on equity is determined solely by its profit margin and how much revenue it can produce from its balance sheet (asset turnover). If it adds debt to its balance sheet, Return on Equity is raised as equity funds less than 100% of the balance sheet assets.

The challenge for the owner (owners) of a company is to determine how much debt can be used to fund the balance sheet without incurring a high risk of bankruptcy or distress due to its inability to service the debt. In the example we've used here, increasing the leverage of XYZ would produce a very significant increase in return on equity.

For example, XYZ produced a 10% ROE with asset turnover of 4.394 profit margin of .02, and leverage of 1.138. Assets are 495 and equity is 435.

Leverage would be higher if the 495 of assets was funded with more debt and less equity. For example, let's reduce equity to 200, substituting it with 235 of debt. Total liabilities would then grow from 60 to 295, and Leverage would increase from 1.138 to 2.475. What is the impact of this on ROE?

If profit margins could be maintained at 2%, the substitution of debt for equity in the balance sheet (increased leverage), results in the ROE growing from 10% to 21.7%

21.75%	=	2.475	X	4.394	X	.02
ROE	=	Leverage	X	Asset Turnover	X	Profit Margin

Of course, it would be more difficult to maintain the 2% profit margin now because the company has just increased one of its major components of expense – interest! But it's possible that management could figure out how to operate a bit more efficiently in order to make up for the increased interest expense. More than likely, profit margins would decrease by all or part of the increased interest expense, and ROE would not be 21.7%, but it would still be a lot higher than it was with much less leverage.

If the management of the company, or its owners, wanted to be very aggressive in terms of leverage, they could produce even an higher ROE. Let's reduce equity to 50, and the 495 of total assets was now funded with 445 of liabilities. We can calculate the amount by which increased interest would reduce operating profits.

In our first example, with low leverage, XYX the supermarket, had revenue of 2175 and pretax profit of 67. Assuming that most of the increased leverage was 9% interest bearing debt of 300 (some of the increased leverage could come from non-interest paying trade payables), the annual interest bill becomes 9% X 300, or 27. This reduces the pretax profit from 67 to 40, and the after tax profit (tax rate of 35%) to 26. The profit margin now becomes 26 / 2175 (total revenue) = 1.195%, down from 2.0% without debt.

But even though the profit margin is reduced, the extraordinary leverage creates an ROE of 52%!

52%	=	9.9	X	4.394	X	.01195
ROE	=	Leverage	X	Asset Turnover	X	Profit Margin

If companies could easily operate, and sustain, this amount of leverage, while producing either high turnover or high margins, they certainly would. It could be a formula for getting very rich! But they can't, for two major reasons.

First, if the business could sustain itself with this leverage, asset turnover, and profit margins, what would logically happen in a competitive environment with little barriers to entry? More competitors would rapidly show up in order to reap such huge returns. And, more competition would drive down profit margins, given the fact that a market can sustain only a certain amount of business. With lower margins, operating profits decrease, cash flow decreases, and this leads to the second reason why high leverage cannot usually be sustained – the bankruptcy risk of financial leverage.

The high interest payments from leverage directly reduce operating profit and margins. This might be fine if revenue, expenses, and operating profits before interest are stable. But in the real world, they are not, for a variety of reasons, competition being only one of them. If revenue should fall, or not grow in line with expenses, operating profit falls very rapidly, and the company is at risk of not being able to meet its interest payments from profits. When this happens, it has to rely on liquidity or the sale of assets to fund the negative profit. By substantially increasing leverage, and reducing the amount of equity that funds the balance sheet, its ability to maintain assets that can quickly be turned into cash, without impairing the business, is very limited. Assets produce revenue, and as assets are liquidated, revenue is usually reduced, as is cash flow. The substantial increase in leverage can severely reduce a company's financial flexibility.

The challenge of creating a company's capital structure is to use enough financial leverage (debt) to achieve an adequate return on equity, as in the models above, without creating too much risk of bankruptcy. The amount of financial leverage that a company can undertake is a function of the nature of its business risks, and the consequent impact on cash flow volatility. The ideal capital structure is one that produces a competitive return on equity, while matching financial risk and business risk.

Capital Structure and Risk

The design of a company's capital structure is not arbitrary. It must be created and maintained to achieve a return on equity that is high enough to attract capital. But it also must be appropriate for the nature of a company's business risk, usually identified as the volatility of its revenue and operating profit, and the resulting cash flow.

Almost every company and every industry has a capital structure that is a natural function of the risks of its business model. This "natural" capital structure is based upon the nature of the assets used to produce revenue and profits, the competitive and regulatory environment, the degree to which it is subject to the macro-economic environment, the labor environment, and the consequent stability of the company's business – revenue and expenses.

Companies that are subject to heavy competition and are highly vulnerable to macro-economic conditions generally cannot survive with a lot of debt – the operating cash flow is subject to a lot of variation (volatility). Companies that are well capitalized (a lot of equity relative to their business risk) can sustain long periods of low or negative cash flow. Companies that are poorly capitalized (too much debt relative to their business risk) cannot sustain long periods of low cash flow before they are forced into bankruptcy by their creditors.

Companies whose assets are highly liquid and have stable value can maintain a lot of leverage. Banks are an example of this. Companies with illiquid assets, but which have very stable revenue and operating costs can also sustain a lot of leverage. Regulated utility companies are an example.

For the past thirty years, private equity firms and investors have been creating huge amounts of wealth (and destroying some as well) through the acquisition of companies using large amounts of debt. The debt is used to buy-out existing owners – public and / or private. In the United States, there was a large boom of these "leverage buy outs" in the 1980's, and again from 2002 through the present. The trend declined during the US recession of the early 1990's, amid a lot of bankruptcies of some of the buy-out deals created in the 1980's.

Many of the deals that didn't work, and ended up in bankruptcy, were the result of adding a lot of debt to the balance sheet (leverage) of companies that could not sustain it, due to high levels of operating risk. Very few bankers or investors ever set out to do a deal that is bound to fail. They never show a business model and cash flow forecast that doesn't work! Projected cash flow will always be shown to be sufficient to reduce debt levels and leverage over time, either from cash flow or from the sale of assets. Usually, projections for increased cash flow are from expected increased operating efficiency and cost reductions.

When these deals don't work out as planned, and the creditors force a bankruptcy, it is often the result of one or both of two factors. Of course one is a general decline in the macro-economic environment (the external factors) that was not anticipated. The other, and the one that is most egregious, is the lack of understanding of the nature of the risks facing the company, and the consequent volatility of its cash flow due to operating and competitive factors. Unfortunately, a lot of smart investors and bankers make this mistake, and continue to do so. One of the key jobs of a credit analyst is to understand which types of business can sustain leverage, and which cannot. This is the concept of the "natural" capital structure.

We will pursue this idea in the next parts of this course. But, here are a couple of examples.

What are the operating risk characteristics of companies in the following industries? What is the degree of volatility of their operating cash flow in a stable economic environment?

Supermarket?
Retail Apparel Department Store Chain?
Software Developer?
Pharmaceutical Manufacturer ?

Supermarket chains have been the subject of a lot of leverage buyouts by private equity investors, and many of them have been successful. The reason is that these businesses have a relatively small degree of revenue and expense volatility. They sell commodity products with relatively stable fixed costs. There is very little inventory risk (the risk that something won't sell at its posted price). When these companies do fail, it's usually do to over-expansion (building new stores that don't produce the anticipated revenue), labor disputes, or extraordinary events, such as a major fire.

Retail apparel chains have also been subject to a lot of buyouts. Most of them failed. Standard and Poor's once wrote a report (after some of the failures) that stated "a highly leverage apparel retailer is a contradiction in terms". There are so many things that can wrong in the business, that high financial leverage adds a huge bankruptcy risk. Merchandise risk is just one of these risks. Moreover, a highly competitive apparel merchandiser needs to have tremendous financial flexibility. They need to move with trends – including buying fresh merchandise and marking down stale merchandise. The investment bankers that structured these deals didn't seem to understand these basic risks.

Are pharmaceutical manufacturing or software development risky businesses? Based on historic knowledge of some very successful companies in these industries, one might be tempted to say "no". But they share a common characteristic that make their business and operating risks very high. Both industries require huge investments in research and development to produce products. The success rate might be relatively low, and the time to develop saleable products can be very long. These industries require a lot of "patient" capital for their business model to work – equity as the dominant part of their capital structure.

The next chapter will review how financial analysis is utilized to assess business risk and capital structure.

Chapter 3

Fundamentals of Financial Analysis

Financial Analysis is the basis for Credit Analysis

"What is the degree of risk that an obligor will have sufficient cash to pay back an obligation when it is due?"

The "art" of credit analysis is to understand how to convert historic financial and operating performance and financial condition information, knowledge of management, and knowledge of industry, into a judgment about an obligor's willingness and ability to repay an obligation in the future.

Financial analysis is the starting point for all "securities" analysis – equity securities and debt (credit) securities or obligations. Historic trends must be examined relative to the current financial position (balance sheet and capital structure) and operating performance. These trends serve as the basis for judging the degree to which forecasts for future operating results and financial position are reasonable.

An equity analyst will use financial analysis tools to estimate the value of a company's equity. Various valuation methods are used, such as price / earnings multiples and the DCF method (discounted cash flow). An equity analyst will use past performance, competitive assessment, management and strategy assessment, and knowledge of the industry to predict future earnings and cash flow.

A credit analyst will use financial analysis to try to establish the degree to which an obligor can fulfill the terms of its debt obligations – short term and long term. This is analogous to the estimation of the value of these obligations. Unlike equity, the value of a debt obligation at its maturity date should be the same as when it was issued. There is no specific maturity date of equity.

Both equity analysis and credit analysis require the use of significant judgment to assess future performance.

This chapter will review how financial analysis is utilized in credit analysis to assess business risk, performance, and capital structure, and the all-important question of "how and when will I get paid back?" Most importantly, it's about identifying the degree of risk associated with the question of "how and when will I get paid back?"

Financial Analysis?

Financial analysis is used to identify and assess all aspects of a company's performance, liquidity, and financial position. It provides some of the information for predicting future performance and financial position.

One of the most valuable benefits of financial analysis is to compare a particular company against its peers – companies in the same or a similar industry. This helps to focus further analysis on areas where a company is at variance from its peers, in terms of operating performance and its capital structure.

Financial analysis is used to determine if a company is funding itself internally from operations, or needs to access external sources of cash. This is a significant aspect of assessing credit risk.

Financial analysis can also be used to determine if operating performance is real; i.e., whether or not there is a chance of fraud in the accounts. The starting point for this is Peer analysis, and the search for "outliers".

Historical financial performance is the starting point for predicting future financial performance. But it is only the starting point. A company's future performance is a function of its industry, competitive situation, its past performance relative to its peers, its management competence, and a comparison of its stated strategy and the analyst's view of the strategic opportunities. As many sorry investors and lenders have learned, the past is not always a guide to the future!

In summary, financial analysis is used to identify and assess:

A company's basic business model – how does it make money? How does it produce an acceptable return on equity? Does it operate with high or low margins? Does it have high or low asset turnover? Does it operate with high or low leverage?

Operating Performance – how is the company doing in terms of profitability? How is it doing in absolute terms and relative to its competitors?

Liquidity – how much cash, or near cash, does the company have relative to its near term financial obligations?

Cash Flow – are a company's operations generating surplus cash, or is it using more cash than it is creating?

Capital Structure – how does the company fund its short-term and long-term assets? How does this compare to its competitors?

Judgments about future performance are clearly based on past performance, but must consider a number of factors that go beyond historic financial analysis. This will be the topic of Chapter 4 – Credit, Risk, Cash Flow and Capital Structure.

Use of Financial Analysis to Understand Company and Industry Business Models

In Chapter 2, we introduced the relationship between a company's operating risks (business risks) and its capital structure. We said that the design of a company's capital structure is not arbitrary. It must be created and maintained to achieve a return on equity that is high enough to attract capital and to create shareholder value. But it also must be appropriate for the nature of a company's business risk.

Almost every company and every industry has a capital structure that is a natural function of the risks of its business model. This "natural" capital structure is based upon the nature of the assets used to produce revenue and profits, the competitive and regulatory environment, the degree to which it is subject to the macro-economic environment, the labor environment, and the consequent stability of the company's business – revenue and expenses.

Companies that are subject to heavy competition and are highly vulnerable to macro-economic conditions generally cannot survive with a lot of debt – the operating cash flow is subject to a lot of variation (volatility). Companies that are well capitalized (a lot of equity relative to their business risk) can sustain long periods of low or negative cash flow. Companies that are poorly capitalized (too much debt relative to their business risk) cannot sustain long periods of low cash flow before they are forced into bankruptcy or forced to restructure.

Companies whose assets are highly liquid and have stable value can maintain a lot of leverage. Banks are an example of this. They are supposed to be an example of this – sometimes they're not! Companies with illiquid assets, but which have very stable revenue and operating costs can also sustain a lot of leverage. Regulated utility companies are an example.

One of the key jobs of a credit analyst is to understand which types of business can sustain leverage, and which cannot. This is the concept of the "natural" capital structure.

What are the operating risk characteristics of companies in the following industries? What is the degree of volatility of their operating cash flow in a stable economic environment?

Supermarket?

Retail Apparel Department Store Chain?
Software Developer?
Pharmaceutical Manufacturer ?

Supermarket chains have been the subject of a lot of leverage buyouts by private equity investors, and many of them have been successful. The reason is that these businesses have a relatively small degree of revenue and expense volatility. They sell commodity products with relatively stable fixed costs. There is very little inventory risk (the risk that something won't sell at its posted price). When these companies do fail, it's usually do to over-expansion (building new stores that don't produce the anticipated revenue), labor disputes, or extraordinary events that disrupt the revenue stream.

Retail apparel chains have also been subject to a lot of buyouts. Most of them failed. Standard and Poor's once wrote a report (after some of the failures) that stated "a highly leverage apparel retailer is a contradiction in terms". There are so many things that can wrong in the business, that high financial leverage adds a huge bankruptcy risk. Merchandise risk is just one of these risks. Moreover, a highly competitive apparel merchandiser needs to have tremendous financial flexibility. They need to move with trends – including buying fresh merchandise and marking down stale merchandise. The investment bankers that structured these deals didn't seem to understand these basic risks.

Are pharmaceutical manufacturing or software development risky businesses? Based on historic knowledge of some very successful companies in these industries, one might be tempted to say "no". But they share a common characteristic that make their business and operating risks very high. Both industries require huge investments in research and development to produce products. The success rate might be relatively low, and the time to develop saleable products can be very long. These industries require a lot of "patient" capital for their business model to work – equity as the dominant part of their capital structure.

As we saw in Chapter 2, the business model of all companies can be defined through the use of the following model....

Return on Equity (ROE) = Profit Margin X Asset Turnover X Leverage

The goal of a company's management is to produce a return on capital that is higher than the alternative of investing in risk free securities (government bonds). Moreover, the return should be adjusted for risk. If management does not produce a return on capital (equity) that is significantly higher than the alternative of investing in a government bond, then it is destroying value. This is the concept of Economic Value Added.

The analysis of how companies make money is the starting point of equity and credit analysis. Financial analysis metrics are underlined in the following descriptions of the business and financial models of a few industries. They are defined later in this Chapter.

Supermarkets tend to have very low profit margins, because they can produce adequate ROE via very high asset turnover. Average days inventory is very low. Leverage is usually moderate, as it is not necessary to employ high leverage for a good ROE due to the high asset turnover. Since the bulk of the assets of a supermarket company tend to be inventory, which is largely financed via credit from vendors, working capital tends to be low, and sometimes negative.

A software developer such as Microsoft or SAP would tend to have high profit margins. It would generally also have low leverage, as the basic nature of its business is very high risk. Product development can take a long time, with very no guarantee of success, and very high fixed costs. The same can be said for the business model of a pharmaceutical manufacturer such as Pfizer or AstraZeneca.

A commercial bank will have very high financial leverage. The nature of a bank's assets are (presumably) of high quality, liquid, and of low risk, which lend them to high leverage financing, and asset turnover is very low, especially if the bank's loans are long term in nature. Banks have extremely low profit margins (spread on loans averaging about 1% for commercial lending, and higher for consumer lending). The only way a bank can produce a return on equity of 10% to 15% is to employ very high leverage.

Definition and use of basic financial ratios

Liquidity – companies become bankrupt when they run out of cash. Two traditional measures of liquidity are the Current Ratio and the Quick Ratio. Both provide an indication of the relationship between a company's cash or "near" cash position, and its obligations that are due in the near future. The quick ratio is the current ration less current assets that are not immediately liquid.

Some companies' liquidity is highly dependent upon short term sources of funding, such as trade credit (accounts payable) or short term bank loans, or lines of credit. A serious question is raised as to whether availability of credit is a source of liquidity. This is a subject for Chapter 3 – Credit Analysis. But please note, that companies who depend upon outside providers of credit, go bankrupt not only because they run out of cash, but also because: they fear that they'll run out of cash, or their suppliers of liquidity fear that they'll run out of cash.

Current Ratio – Current assets / Current liabilities. This is a basic measure of liquidity. A low or even negative current ratio is an indication that a company is heavily dependent on short term sources of funding, which can be transient and evaporate. A company could become insolvent very quickly if a creditor declines to continue to provide short term funding, particularly if the short term assets (current assets) are not extremely liquid.

Quick Ratio - cash, marketable securities and accounts receivable / current liabilities. This is a more refined measure of liquidity than the current ratio. It excludes current assets that cannot be turned into cash in a relatively short period of time.

Inventory turnover is a very important measure of asset efficiency (asset productivity). Competing companies in an industry should have similar turnover ratios. If there is an outlier, it could be an indicator of a potential problem, or competitive advantage.

Receivables collection period (days receivable) is another way to compare the operations of two competing companies in the same industry. It is also important to examine this over time for trends, good or bad. A lengthening collection period could be an indicator of deteriorating quality of the accounts receivable, or sloppy collection management.

Leverage ratios are a key indicator of financial risk. A basic measure of leverage is the ratio of total equity to total assets. This describes the portion of total assets that are funded by equity vs liabilities. Other typical metrics for leverage are: total debt / equity, total debt / total assets (which is the inverse of equity/assets), and long term debt / total capitalization.

Interest coverage is a metric that assesses the relationship between a company's gross cash flow and its periodic interest payments. This is a particularly important metric for highly leveraged companies. There are some arbitrary market standards for coverage, by debt rating, but it is important that all fixed obligations (interest, principle payments, taxes, and capital expenditures) are reviewed relative to a company's earnings. Gross earnings for this measurement are sometimes referred to as "EBITDA" – earnings before interest, taxes, depreciation and amortization. EBITDA is a proxy for gross cash flow.

Measures of Operating Performance include metrics that identify how a company is performing for its owners (Return on Equity), and how it is performing relative to its competitors (Profit Margin). As we've discussed, Return on Equity (ROE) is net profit / equity. Usually this ratio will use average equity, not the equity amount at the end of a particular fiscal period. Profit Margin is net profit / sales.

In addition, a financial analyst will need to understand how a company makes money. It might sell its products for a very high gross margin (selling price minus cost of goods sold). If that's the case, it might have a lot of flexibility regarding operating expenses. The net profit margin is the result of the combination of the gross margin, and the expense margin. The size of the gross margin is usually determined by competitive factors. The expense margin or operating margin (sales and operating expense / sales) is under management control. If a company operates with a thin gross margin, it must control expenses very carefully, and a financial analyst will monitor the expense margin. In a competitive industry "the low cost producer, wins"! This is a ratio that a credit analyst will monitor carefully over time, as discussed in the next chapter.

Operating Leverage is a basic corporate finance and micro-economic concept. It refers to the degree that a company has high or low fixed expenses relative to revenue. If all of a company's expenses are variable, they are highly correlated with sales, and the operating margin will be relatively stable regardless of the level of sales. Expenses go up and down with sales volumes.

Industry Analysis and Structure

All industries have financial characteristics that are driven by the nature of their business. All companies within an industry will tend to have common financial characteristics – both the balance sheet and the income statement. Competition will drive profit margins among competitors, and the operating risks of an industry will drive the composition of the balance sheet. Industry practices will determine how much funding is supplied by vendors, and how much by debt and equity. A peer analysis of companies within an industry will lead to the identification of "outliers", which are certain financial indicators that are different from peers, and which require investigation to determine why. Sometimes the answer is logical, due to management or a particular situation. Sometimes the answer is not clear, which should lead to a sense of skepticism about whether or not the situation is correctly portrayed by the financial statements and statistics.

In peer analysis, one of the first questions to ask is "how is the company performing?" The ratio that gives the first indication of this is "net income / net worth", which is the Return on Equity. An analyst would expect a well performing company to produce an ROE in the range of 10% - 20%. Anything above or below that is an indicator of an 'outlier" – something to be explored to determine why performance is above or below average. It may an industry issue, or it may be unique to the company.

The next step in peer analysis might be to use financial ratios to understand the business model of how the company produces its Return on Equity (ROE). As noted, ROE is a direct, mathematical, function of three elements – profit margin, asset productivity, and leverage. Profit margin is net income / sales or turnover. Asset productivity is the ratio of sales or turnover to total assets. Leverage is the ratio of total assets to equity.

For example, take a company with very low asset productivity (net sales / assets = 3%), very high leverage (total assets / net worth = 18.5, or the inverse, net worth / total assets = 5.48%. It also has very good profit margins (about 31%). This combination of low asset productivity, good profit margins, and high leverage, produces an ROE of 17%.

(Asset Productivity) X (Leverage) X (Profit Margin) = Return on Equity
        (.03)   X   (18.5)   X   (.31) = .17 = 17% ROE

Another company has very low profit margins (net profit / net sales =3.3%), but produces very good ROE (18.3%) via relatively high asset productivity (sales / total assets = 2.28), and moderate leverage (total assets / net worth = 2.46).

For companies with very high leverage, one of the questions the credit analyst must answer is "is this leverage sustainable", or does it present a degree of risk that is not compatible with the company's (or industry's) business risk (which we also describe as volatility of cash flow).

Companies and industries have business models that are driven by the nature of what they do and the competitive situation in their industry. The balance sheet is unique to each business model – it is a function of the risks of the business, the funding sources available to the particular industry, and the means by which the company generates revenue.

The primary source of revenue for a commercial bank is the "spread" on loans – the difference between the net revenue rate it receives on loans and its cost of funding. Net revenue is interest received less loan losses. This spread, or net interest margin, is relatively small. Perhaps 1% of a loan for a large corporate borrower, or as much as 6% for a consumer type of loan. This results in very low asset productivity, as measured by the ratio of net sales to total assets. Other sources of revenue for a bank are fees and trading income.

A bank's profit margin is the ratio of its non-interest expenses (salaries, premises, operations, taxes, etc.) to total revenue. This is generally in the range of 25% to 30%. So, in order to produce an ROE in the range of 15% (after tax), a bank must operate with very high leverage, since its asset productivity is extraordinarily low, and profit margins are moderate.

A discount retailer will operate with very low profit margins. That's the basis for its competitive position. Its business risk is relatively high, as it is subject to macro-economic trends, and it does not sell products that are easily differentiated. Leverage tends to be relatively low for companies in this industry. Therefore, in order to produce a competitive ROE, these companies must have extremely high asset productivity, as seen in the ratio of sales to total assets. It also makes sense that a discount store would have rapid inventory turnover, particularly if it is selling grocery items as well as soft goods. A key success factor for a discount retailer is high inventory turnover.

Software development and pharmaceutical development and manufacturing are industries with a lot in common. While the products produced have very little in common, the risks of these industries are relatively similar. Both industries depend on intensive, and expensive, R&D to develop products. The outcome of this R&D is never certain, nor is the timing. Companies in these industries operate with very high fixed costs, and very high business risk. They must have a lot of "patient" capital to cover the investment period before their successful products produce revenue. They tend to have relatively high profit margins. When a product is successful, it tends to have pricing strength in the market, with little marginal cost of production. Most of the product costs are in the R&D effort. A software company probably does not have as much investment in plant and equipment as would a pharmaceutical manufacturer. Acquisition of other companies are common in these two industries, which would be reflected in a relatively large proportion of intangible assets (goodwill) to total assets.

Airlines and electric utility companies have a common characteristic – very high investments in fixed plant and equipment. These are fixed asset intensive companies, with only moderate asset productivity (sales relative to total assets are low). In order to produce a good ROE, these companies must generate high profit margins or use a lot of leverage. High leverage for an electric utility is not necessarily bad, as its cash flow is relatively stable, especially if it's regulated. Unregulated airlines have a very difficult time generating stable cash flow!

Inventory turnover and the ratio of inventory to total assets are very useful statistics for identifying an industry. Obviously a bank would not have a lot of inventory relative to total assets, nor would an airline or a software developer. A discount retailer would not have a lot of accounts receivable, unless it maintained its own private label credit card.

Trend Analysis – Making Judgments and Early Warning Signs

A common mistake of an inexperienced financial analysis is to write a review of a company's historical performance in the form of "elevator analysis". This is a review that consists primarily of statements about certain parameters going "up" or "down", but without any insights provided about "why" or the significance of the trend.

Trend analysis of financial statements is very important, but only useful if an analyst can identify significance to the trends, and causality. The purpose of trend analysis is to identify factors that imply superb performance, or factors that are warning signs.

An equity analyst is trying to establish the value of a company based on the present value of future cash flows. Earnings are a proxy for cash flow, and historical performance is the starting point, but only the starting point, for predicting future performance.

A credit analyst is trying to judge a company's ability to pay back its short term, and long term, obligations. Since earnings are a proxy for cash flow, the analyst will look at the historical stability, or growth, in earnings to help predict future earnings. But, the credit analyst must also carefully examine trends in balance sheet items and net cash flow to identify potential cash or liquidity problems. Of course, this must include debt repayment obligations.

In terms of operations, it is important to look at trends in gross margins and operating margins. Good gross margins, along with good net margins, might hide a growing expense problem that will eventually result in reduced net (profit) margins. Net margins could be stable, or even growing, while operating expense margins are deteriorating. This could occur if gross margins were improving to make up for the increased relative operating expenses.

Inventory turnover ratio is a very important trend to monitor, for both the equity analyst and the credit analyst. Declining inventory turnover could be an indication of products that aren't selling well, and markdowns or inventory write downs that will have to be recognized at some point in the near future.

Increasing days receivable could be an indication of deteriorating credit from customers, or a change in selling terms to maintain sales in a deteriorating market.

The ultimate goal of all of this analysis is to assess a company's current and future liquidity, which is the basis for servicing its debt obligations.

Cash Flow Analysis – Introduction

A credit analyst will perform many of the same financial analysis tasks as an equity analyst. The goals are similar – to predict future cash flow.

The equity analyst is working to establish value, usually based upon the present value of future cash flows. Future earnings are often used as a proxy for future cash flows.

The credit analyst is working to determine the degree to which a company is able to service its debt in the near term and in the future. Cash flow forecasting is part of this task. Future net cash flow generation, after all other fixed obligations, including capital expenditure, must be compared to future interest and principle obligations.

But a credit analyst must also be able to examine current liquidity. He or she must also be able to understand historical cash generation, and the means by which a company has been funding its assets. There are many cases of company failures that were missed by analysts and bankers because they missed a simple fact that the company's cash flow was not sufficient to fund asset growth, even though it may be been reporting profits. Enron is an excellent example of this. Enron appeared to be an extremely profitable company, almost up to the point of its bankruptcy. But it was not generating sufficient cash from its operations to fund its growth. In the two years prior to its demise, Enron had negative cash flow in the range of $2 billion. This was all funded by debt. This was exacerbated by the fact that a lot of this debt was hidden from analysts and investors via off balance sheet vehicles.

Cash flow analysis for credit analysis is the topic of Chapters 4 and 6.

Chapter 4

Credit, Risk, Cash Flow, and Capital Structure

"Lending is not based primarily on money or property. No sir, the first thing is character" – J.P. Morgan

The goal of credit analysis is to make a judgment about an obligor's ability and willingness to pay back what it owes, when it is owed. This means that the analyst must understand all of the issues raised by Mr. Morgan – money, property, and character.

A credit analyst will perform many of the same financial analysis tasks as an equity analyst. The goals are similar – to understand the basis for historic performance and to predict future cash flow. The equity analyst is working to establish value, usually based upon the present value of future cash flows. Future earnings are often used as a proxy for future cash flows.

The credit analyst is working to determine the degree to which a company is able to service its debt in the near term and in the future. Historic cash flow analysis and forecasting is the means of achieving this. Estimated future net cash flow, and the risks associated with that estimate, is the basis for establishing the probability that the obligor will be able to service its debt.

In order to understand a company's ability to generate cash to service debt in the future, it is necessary to understand historic cash generation, and the means by which a company has been funding its assets.

There are many cases of company failures that were missed by analysts and bankers because they ignored a simple fact that the company's cash flow had not been sufficient to fund asset growth, even though it may be been reporting profits.

Enron is an excellent example of this. Enron appeared to be an extremely profitable company, almost up to the point of its bankruptcy. But it was not generating sufficient cash from its operations to fund its growth. In the two years prior to its demise, Enron had negative cash flow, after investments, in the range of $2 billion. This was all funded by debt. Enron's problem was exacerbated by the fact that a lot of this debt was hidden from analysts and investors via off balance sheet vehicles. Its immediate cause of bankruptcy was the loss of confidence by its suppliers of credit. Once they understood that Enron's leverage was much higher than many realized, the creditors refused to continue to work with the company.

It is possible that Enron was a viable company prior to its bankruptcy. The immediate cause of its rapid failure was that the suppliers of credit to Enron feared that it was going to run out of cash very quickly. They "ran for the exits".

"What is the degree of risk that an obligor will have sufficient cash to pay back an obligation on a timely basis, and the willingness to do so?"

If the obligation is short term, and the obligor has a lot of liquidity, the answer is probably easy to determine. If the time frame is longer, the answer is not so easy. The credit analyst must assess many factors that will impact the obligor's ability to pay in the future, including the willingness to pay. If a confident conclusion cannot be reached, the transaction will be rejected, or structured to reduce the risks, usually through the taking of collateral or security (a "second way out").

If a creditor doesn't have a lot of confidence in the identified means of getting paid back (the "first way out"), then it will look to a back-up means of getting paid back (the "second way out") – perhaps in the form of additional collateral or a third party guarantee.

In modern risk management, the degree of risk relative to a specific obligor or obligation is usually expressed in the form of a quantitative <u>risk rating</u>. This is analogous to a <u>debt rating</u> from a rating agency. Risk ratings or debt ratings provide the basis for modern credit risk portfolio management in financial institutions. They are intended to provide a quantification of the probability of an obligor's risk of default.

The concept of capital structure has also been introduced. Companies that operate in high risk industries have volatile operating cash flow. To avoid the risk of bankruptcy or insolvency, they need to be financed with "patient" forms of capital, which means equity or equity like instruments. These forms of capital have no set date for repayment, and the dividends, if any, can be suspended. Companies with low operating risk tend to have relatively stable cash flow, and can assume a lot of debt with little risk of insolvency. A "strong" capital structure implies that a company can liquidate assets to finance negative operating cash flow in situations where it is not able to borrow to do so.

An all too common mistake of bankers, and investors, has been to assist and/or allow companies with very high business and operating risk, to assume a lot of financial risk in the form of leverage. Because these companies have volatile operating cash flow, over time they are at high risk of not being able to meet their fixed cash expenses, including debt service. Unless they can figure out how to de-leverage very quickly, usually through the sale of assets, they will have a difficult time surviving. Sometimes these highly leveraged companies will reduce expenses drastically to produce more cash flow. And, sometimes this works. Unfortunately, it can also destroy a company's ability to compete, which then results in reduced revenue, reduced cash flow, and eventually bankruptcy.

A critically important role of financial analysis is to determine the nature of a company's business model, and how it uses its balance sheet and capital structure to produce income and an acceptable return on capital. The business model and performance must also be reasonable relative to competitors in its industry. Any "outliers" in performance or capital structure require further analysis to explain the differences. A leading indicator of possible fraud is an inability to explain much better performance than peers, or a very different capital structure.

A company's capital structure represents the relationship between the level of its debt and its equity in the funding of its assets. The nature of the capital structure and the balance between debt and equity is determined by the degree of stability or instability of net operating cash flow.

An obligor's debt capacity (companies as well as consumers) is primarily a function of its future cash flow. Predicting future cash flow, and its degree of volatility or stability, is fundamental to the art of credit analysis.

Principles of Credit – How do Creditors get Paid Back?

In the process of credit analysis, and equity analysis, judgments and predictions must be made about future performance and cash flow. This is done in the context of:

- historic performance,
- current financial position, capital structure and liquidity
- management capability,
- business strategy
- competitors' performance,
- competitive pressure,
- the nature of the industry and forces at work
- the macro-economic environment.

And, as indicated by the quote from J.P. Morgan, a judgment must also be made about an obligor's integrity and willingness to fulfill its obligations.

The basic principles of extending credit are the same for all types of borrowers – corporate, consumer, and financial institutions. The credit analyst is trying to answer the basic question: "what is the risk of being repaid on a timely basis, in accordance with the terms of the obligation?" Or, simply stated, "how and when am I going to get paid back, and by whom?"

If you have absolute and confirmed faith in your obligor, then it's easy to understand how to get paid back – it's "trust". But there are times when even the most "trustworthy" obligor makes a mistake. Character is important, but it is incumbent on every credit analyst to understand the means by which the obligor is going to fulfill an obligation. The analyst also has to judge whether or not the means of repayment is reasonable – does it make sense? The will to repay may exist, but it can't happen if the means is not there!

Also, in modern risk management, the credit analyst must make a quantifiable assessment of the degree of "reasonableness" of getting repaid. This is in the form of estimating a relative probability of default in the form of a risk rating or a debt rating. The rating serves as the basis for managing portfolios of risk comprised of many obligors.

Obligations are repaid from cash. The ability of a borrower, corporate or consumer, to pay back an obligation is a function of either cash on hand (or liquidity in the form of "near cash" assets) or the generation of cash.

Cash to repay obligations comes from only four possible sources:

- existing cash or very liquid investments
- cash flow from operating income (less expenses and investments),
- the sale or liquidation of assets, or
- external sources (guarantors, new equity or refinancing).

Borrowers become insolvent and go bankrupt for one or all of three reasons, all related to cash:

- They run out of cash
- They fear that they will run out of cash, and wish to protect what they have, or
- Their external suppliers of credit fear that they will run out of cash and wish to stop any further cash "burn". These creditors can force bankruptcy.

Companies usually run out of cash due to a combination of poor operating performance and too much debt. In rare cases it is due to fraud on the part of management. The job of the credit analyst is to figure out if or when this might happen.

The ability to service debt obligations is primarily about cash and collateral. But as noted by J.P. Morgan, it also is about character. An obligor dedicated to fraud has a substantial advantage over a credit analyst, but not a total advantage. One of the roles of a credit analyst is to sense the possibility of fraud, either via financial analysis, or by an assessment of the character traits and history of the borrower. In compliance terms, this is referred to as "know your borrower".

Chapter 5

Principles of Extending Credit - Consumer Credit, Corporate Credit, and Financial Institution Credit

The principles of the extension of credit are fundamentally the same regardless of the nature of the obligor – consumer, commercial, or financial institution. The goal is to have the obligation repaid as anticipated, from the obvious sources – cash on hand, cash flow from operating income, cash from the sale of an asset, or cash from an outside party providing payment.

One of the lessons of the credit crisis of 2007 / 2008 is that all types of risk converge and are, fundamentally, credit risk – the risk that an obligor will fulfill its commitment to a creditor on a timely basis.

The trading desks of financial institutions tend to focus on "market risk" – the risk of the change in price of a marketable security. However, as has been experienced in 2007 and 2008, when liquidity in markets dries up, market risk becomes credit risk. A security which is tradable, but subject to market price fluctuations, becomes a security to be held to maturity when there is no longer a liquid market for its sale as a trading asset. In that case, the holder of the security will be paid only when the issuer of the security pays at maturity. If the security cannot be sold in the market, the owner of the security is taking the credit risk of the obligor who issued the security.

Global financial innovation in banking and corporate finance has created multiple ways of distributing risk and hedging risk. This has been applied to consumer credit and corporate credit. Bank loans are now distributed to investors via securitization. In 2007, the credit crisis arose from the fact that consumer mortgages were being originated and funded outside of the banking system. Loans were originated by mortgage brokers rather than banks, and then packaged and sold to investors via securitizations known as "CDO's" – Collateralized Debt Obligations.

The CDO's began to experience problems when the default rates on the mortgages in the portfolios exceeded expected amounts. The ultimate cause of this was weak credit standards and analysis in the origination of the mortgages in the portfolio. The crisis was caused by inadequate credit underwriting – consumers were given mortgages that they couldn't afford, and the value of the residences secured by the mortgages were not sufficient to pay off the mortgages. This apparently was not well understood by the bankers who created many of these CDO's, nor by the investors who bought them. The cause of the losses incurred by owners of these securities was ultimately credit risk of the obligors on the mortgages.

Consumer Credit

"Apply for a mortgage in the UK these days with less than a 10 per cent deposit and chances are the computer will say no." Financial Times (3 April, 2008)

As implied in this quote, most consumer credit decisions are based upon statistical models.

Consumer loans are small relative to most corporate loans. Consequently, creditors cannot afford to pursue much more than basic information and insights about a potential borrower. There isn't enough profit from most consumer loans to pay for it.

In countries with large consumer finance businesses, lenders rely on limited personal information, public data bases, and statistical models to make their decisions. Basic information is collected, such as income level, fixed expenses, stability of income (work history), life stability (stable residency, for example), and credit history (timeliness of payments, payment defaults, lawsuits, etc.). A model will provide a "credit score" and a decision will be made relative to this statistic and the lender's own appetite for risk. Loan underwriting standards will be set according to the lender's appetite for risk, competition, and the economic environment.

The subprime mortgage fiasco of 2007 / 2008 was the result of a number of factors. But the underlying issue was the fact that portfolios of these loans ended up with default rates that were much higher than predicted by historic statistical models.

In retrospect, it appears as though credit underwriting criteria became very liberal, with little concern about the amount of leverage incurred by the obligor, or the amount and quality of the income. The rationale for the mortgage loans, both "prime" and "subprime" was that the value of the property being financed would continue to rise, and the equity of the owner would build. Default rates would be low due to the increase in the value of the property. There was an assumption that the housing "bubble" would not burst.

There also may have been situations where the model credit scores of potential buyers were unrealistically high due to aggressive, and perhaps misleading, estimates of incomes.

The concept of "sub-prime" is one where a borrower has a very weak credit history, possibly combined with a loan size that is very large relative to income or anticipated income. In other words, a "sub-prime" borrower is one of marginal credit quality. This might be for a number of reasons, but it was usually due to low or instable income relative to the size of the mortgage loan. Many of these borrowers couldn't afford the homes they were buying and the related mortgage loans. Their projected cash flow from reported sources of income, relative to their expenses, was barely, if at all, able to service the mortgage payments. In some cases, the borrowers might also have had a poor credit payment history – late payments or defaulted payments.

In many cases, cash flow for loan repayment was ignored. In many markets, there seems to have been an assumption that the price of homes would rise on a consistent basis, and that loans would be repaid from the sale of residences at a profit, or the refinancing. Unlike traditional residential mortgage loans, repayment from the obligor's cash flow was not a significant consideration.

This is invariably a lending strategy that leads to losses if the fundamental assumption is wrong. This is "one way out lending". The payback of the loan is only from one possible source, and if the assumptions about the source or value of the "way out" are incorrect, there's no other way of getting paid in full.

In many "sub-prime" mortgage portfolios, many of the borrowers probably didn't have sufficient cash flow to service their mortgage debt over time. The "first way out" was the increase in the value of the home to the extent that it could be sold at a profit by the borrower, or, if the borrower defaulted on the debt, it could be sold by the lender at a profit. There was no "second way out". Since the borrower probably couldn't make the mortgage payments over time, the only "way out" was the sale of the property. As the real estate bubble burst, the market values not only didn't climb, they fell. Of course one of the reasons they fell was the fact that the values were inflated due to the ability of buyers (borrowers) to bid up the price of homes because financing was readily available, at almost any price, with no restraints due to credit underwriting standards. Very liberal lending standards provided the fuel for the housing bubble.

"One way out" loans tend to be the downfall of bankers. It is possible to structure a "one way out" loan with a very high probability of being paid. But the risks associated with assumptions and structure must be very well understood and managed. Even loans secured by cash sometimes default – the explanation is the subject for a legal textbook!

As with the case of the sub-prime consumer mortgage crisis, there are many cases of well intentioned "one way out" corporate loans where the assumptions turn out to be very incorrect. A common case is a loan made to a company based upon a "market takeout" – proceeds from a public debt offering or from the issuance of common stock. If the only way out of the private loan is a public security sale, this is evidence of the "greater fool" theory. If the company cannot produce sufficient cash flow to repay a private loan, then there is a decent chance that other investors, through the public market, might be skeptical about achieving their desired return!

Commercial and Corporate Credit

Assessing the risk of repayment of a commercial obligation is much more difficult than that of a consumer loan – the corporation doesn't receive a paycheck every week! In effect, the job of the corporate credit analyst is to assess what the size of that "paycheck" will be relative to its cash expenditures (i.e., net cash flow), and the degree to which it is stable or not.

The type and form of extension of commercial credit is very broad, as are the providers of credit and the nature of the obligors. While the basic analysis is the same for all types of credit extension – determining the risk of getting paid back on time – the degree of analysis does vary in accordance with the nature of the extension of credit, and the goals of the creditor.

Companies finance their assets (operations) with a combination of credit and equity. The vast majority of commercial operations around the world depend upon private sources of financing. They don't have access to public capital markets. Equity comes from their owners, and credit comes from a variety of private sources. Even very large companies still depend upon private sources for a significant proportion of their financing. In countries where there are developed capital markets, a certain proportion of companies have access to funds via these capital markets – debt and equity.

Some forms of credit arise in the natural course of business. Suppliers of merchandise will often deliver before payment, landlords will accept rent payments in arrears, and employees provide their services in advance.

Each of these has a potential risk of repayment, and will make a judgment about the ability and willingness of the obligor to make its payments when due. If there is lack of confidence in the obligor's ability or willingness to pay, then it is natural to minimize this risk. Merchandise suppliers will demand cash on delivery or a letter of credit, landlords might demand a deposit of a certain amount of the rent. Employees might demand to be paid daily or weekly. Each of these creditors must make a decision about the degree of risk associated with their extension of credit to their obligor.

As businesses become larger, commercial banks become significant suppliers of short term credit for these "working capital" needs. Inventory is financed beyond the period available from merchandise suppliers, and accounts receivable are financed as companies provide credit on the terms of sale to their own customers. These working capital loans are generally unsecured, but if there is significant concern about the near term solvency of an obligor, then inventory and accounts receivable can be financed on a commercial finance basis. The lender will take the assets as collateral, and only lend against a proportion of the estimated value.

Large companies with access to capital markets will borrow short term through a number of vehicles. Commercial paper is one of the most common. Average maturities are very short (1 – 15 days). Commercial paper lenders are extremely risk adverse, and depend upon commercial banks to pay the notes at maturity if the lender cannot, or if the paper cannot be refinanced due to market illiquidity.

Long term debt and credit is extended to companies by banks, government agencies, and a variety of private investors, including pension funds and insurance companies. Again, if there is access to capital markets, companies can issue notes and bonds to investors.

In each case of credit extension, the creditor is making a risk decision about the issuer of the obligation. The goals are the same – establishing the degree of risk that an obligation will be repaid in accordance with its terms.

Different creditors have different degrees of appetite for risk. Risk is priced accordingly. Another goal of credit analysis is to ensure that the creditor is being paid an appropriate rate of return for the degree of risk undertaken.

Financial Institutions Credit

Financial Institutions are all about credit! Banks and insurance companies require a great deal of leverage in order to produce an adequate return to their shareholders. But, the nature of the businesses, and the nature of the assets allow for this. This was a key part of Lessons I and II of this course.

The analysis of the risks of extending credit to financial institutions (banks, investment banks, hedge funds) is also known as "counter-party" risk analysis. Banks borrow funds from the public and from other financial institutions. Trading and treasury operations of banks, brokers and insurance companies deal in huge amounts of short and long term transactions involving cash funds and derivatives. Each transaction, regardless of tenor, requires an assessment of the risk that the obligation will be repaid in accordance with its terms.

Some of these risks are covered, and collateralized, entirely by the asset being traded. In 2007 we learned the lesson that assumptions about "marketability" and market price of collateral are not always valid! Liquid securities becoming illiquid was at the heart of 2008 global credit crisis.

As we saw in the demise of the U.S. investment bank, Bear Stearns, continued market confidence, trust, and liquidity, are critical to the survival of even large and highly regarded and rated banks. This is an example of a situation where the risks of short term exposure are highly correlated to the risks of long term survival. The US rating agency, Moody's, suggests that because it is so difficult to analyze a financial institution, the most important factor in the long term debt rating is the viability of its business model, the competence of management, and the ability to generate good and consistent earnings over time. This is sometimes referred to as the "franchise" value. Short term lenders are always vulnerable to the long term prospects and credit worthiness of a borrower. This is why one of the age old principles of credit extension is: "Don't lend short term if you're not willing to lend long term."

Types of Corporate Credit and Financing

The extension of credit to companies has many purposes. The most traditional, and most common, is for working capital – short term assets such as inventory and account receivable. As noted above, it is provided by suppliers, banks, and finance companies.

Long term credit is used primarily for investment in plant and equipment, although there are many conceivable needs for funding that has a maturity in excess of one year.

All credit obligations must eventually be settled or repaid. While many times an obligation is refinanced, or extended, there must be an ultimate ability to settle in cash. That's what a credit analyst is trying to determine.

Financing Based Upon Cash Flow – short term and long term

Short term debt is commonly thought of as debt that matures in less than one year. In reality, its maturity is usually much less than one year. Debt in the form of credit from trade suppliers is usually due in 30 to 90 days from delivery. Short term bank debt can be payable "on demand", but more often than not will have notes that mature in 30 to 90 days. For large companies with access to the public commercial paper market (CP), the maturities are usually less than 30 days. Short term debt is often "rolled over" or extended. But if the holder of the debt demands payment, this will come from a company's liquidity. Either from cash on hand, or the natural cash generated from the collection of accounts receivable or the liquidation of inventory.

For the extension of credit for relatively short term periods, cash from operations and cash from the sale of assets are often fundamentally the same. Seasonal agricultural loans are a centuries old example of this.

A loan is made to a farmer in the spring, and repaid from the proceeds of the sale of the harvested crop in the fall. In this case, cash flow from operations is also the same as cash from the sale of assets – the crops. In a good year, there will be something left over for the farmer. In a bad year, there may not be sufficient cash to repay the loan; the lender will have to wait (and hope) for a great crop the next year. All of a sudden, a short term loan can become a longer term loan. This is the meaning of an old banking aphorism "never lend short where you'd not be willing to lend long".

This is also analogous to lending to a merchandise wholesaler, though the inventory cycle may be less seasonable. Loans are made to finance the purchase of inventory, and repaid when the merchandise is sold. In reality, businesses are not totally seasonal, and loans to finance inventory are often (usually) "rolled over" and remain outstanding. But, one of the goals of short term credit analysis is to make sure that the loan to finance inventory can (and will) be repaid if inventory levels fall due to reduced business volume or a change in the business. Unfortunately, what often happens is that the value of inventory also falls when business volumes fall, and the cash value may or may not be sufficient to pay off the loan made to fund the inventory. In that case, the lender of a short term loan (to finance inventory), becomes a long term lender dependent upon the overall cash flow of the business to be repaid.

The principles of providing credit to an agricultural business are absolutely the same as providing credit to businesses in any industry. The differences lie in understanding the business dynamics and risks that drive the industry.

A good agricultural lender will look to a farmer's short term and long term prospects. The lender will have to estimate crop prices at the harvest, look at prospects for the volume of the harvest (including the weather forecast!), and make a judgment about how well the farmer operates the business, as well as his history of performance. Hopefully this will result in an estimate that, after the sale of the harvest and operating expenses, there will be enough cash left over to pay back the "seasonal" loan.

But just in case there won't be enough cash at the end of the season, the lender must take a longer view, and estimate the farmer's ability to generate enough cash in the long term to repay any balance that might be left over from this year's loan, and the loan that will have to be made to finance the following year's crop. If the lender is not willing to provide financing for the next year, the farmer is out of business, and the lender loses money.

As with the short term decision, the lender will need to make a judgment about the farmer's operating efficiency, work ethic, and moral character. The lender will also have to make a judgment about crop prices in the future, as well as long term weather trends. The process of making a judgment about whether or not a farmer can pay back a seasonal loan becomes very complicated!

If the lender has an excellent long term weather forecast, and fears that there may be a long period of "bad crop years", or if there is concern that any of the other factors might impair the generation of sufficient cash, he or she may want another, non-operating source of repayment. This is sometimes referred to as a "second way out" or secondary source of cash generation to repay an obligation. It usually is in the form of the potential sale of an asset with an estimated value. If the lender is very concerned, and if the legal environment permits it, the lender might take a specific pledge of an asset that would be transferred to the lender and sold if the loan defaults. For an agricultural loan, the assets pledged would include equipment and land.

Most long term loans or other types of long term obligations will be repaid from the generation of operating cash flow; i.e., revenue (operating income) less cash expenses (outflows).

Long term debt is usually in the form of bank term loans or publicly or privately placed long term notes or bonds. This debt may be amortizing (period payments of principle) or be due in a lump sum at maturity. Most bank terms loans require periodic principal payments.

Public and privately placed notes and bonds often have a single payment due at maturity. Repayment of long term debt comes from annual cash flow generation or refinancing. But, refinancing of long term debt will occur only if the lender is confident that the borrower has the ability to generate cash flow to repay it, or the ability to sell large amounts of assets to repay.

The lender of long term funds must make a judgment about the obligor's ability to generate sufficient cash flow in the future to meet all of its needs, including debt service. How to do this is the subject of Lesson IV.

Financing based upon the Sale or Liquidation of Assets

In some cases, a credit transaction may be structured such that the liquidation of collateral is the "only way out." Often the extension of credit in the securities industry is done only on the basis of "margin" – credit is extended to finance a portion of the purchase price of a security. If the market value falls, the obligor must provide additional cash or collateral. If the obligor doesn't do this, the credit has the right to sell the security. This may or may not be done with any recourse to the obligor if there's a loss on the liquidation of the security.

There are many instances of lending where cash flow for the repayment of a loan is solely from the sale of an asset. Much of the banking industry and hedge fund industry is financed in this manner. Loans are made by banks and other lenders to finance the purchase and hold of financial instruments. These loans are made at a certain percentage of the market value of the asset, which is usually established on a daily basis (if not more often). If the value falls below a certain amount, the borrower is asked to make up the difference with cash (often referred to as "margin"). If the borrower fails to do so, the lender has the right to sell the asset. Of course, this is the same principle as lending to individuals against the value of their investments in common stocks – margin lending.

The financial markets are dependent on this type of financing of marketable securities. The credit crisis of 2008 has resulted in a loss of confidence in the ability to value some financial instruments. As a result, lenders have been unwilling to provide financing that in the past has been routine. The problem is the inability to value assets, not the credit quality of the borrower.

However, if lenders believe that a borrower has a large concentration of hard to value assets relative to its capital, they may not be willing to extend credit of any nature. If the capital gets wiped out through the fall in value of assets, then borrower is literally out of business. Any lender who didn't get the extra collateral when the margin call was made, becomes a long term lender.

This is analogous to the farmer who can't pay off the seasonal crop loan. The lender will be repaid only if the farmer stays in business and has one or more very good years. Again, the phrase comes into play of an old banker – "never lend short where you wouldn't lend long".

A significant amount of commercial lending around the world is done via asset based finance. Commercial finance specialists establish procedures to create low risk lending situations based entirely on the cash flow from the liquidation of accounts receivable and inventory. They even make very low risk loans to companies in bankruptcy! The loans fund very liquid assets and the bankruptcy judge gives the lender has first priority on the cash from the liquidation of the assets, which are usually accounts receivable.

Other specialized lenders provide financing solely on the value of equipment. To be successful, they must have a superb understanding of the value and marketability of the equipment, and operate in a legal environment that enables them to take the equipment in the event of a default by the borrower. Many airplanes and ships are financed in this manner.

Financing based upon repayment from a third party

There are many situations where there is a need for credit but local providers of financing decide that the risk of being repaid is too high to accept, or that they are not in a position to assess the risk. But, there may be an outside party that has a vested interest in the borrower and the need for financing, or is in a better position to assess the risk. In these cases, they are often willing to provide a guarantee or other form of support to encourage the lender to provide the financing. The risk is shifted largely from the creditor to the third party. The first from of repayment is still the cash flow of the borrower, but the risk of repayment, is born by the third party.

Many government infrastructure projects, such as toll roads, are seemingly viable projects, but the ultimate amount of future cash flow is very difficult to determine due to the extraordinarily high types of risks encountered. As projects are developed and built, many things can go wrong, and the ultimate generation of cash flow is subject to changing economic conditions and competitive factors. The Eurotunnel is an example of a project that has continuously failed to meet the cash flow generation estimates.

Because infrastructure projects presumably have general benefits to the public, and contribute to economic growth and development, financing is usually provided, at least in part, by public funding or development institutions (such as the EBRD, the World Bank, etc.). Government guarantees also provide the comfort to financial institutions to provide financing.

The history of global trade rests upon the concept of the bank Letter of Credit. Suppliers in one country had (and have) little ability to judge the credit strength of buyers in another country, or sometimes in the same country. If the purchaser's bank is willing to provide credit, the bank will issue a Letter of Credit to the seller, thus transferring the credit risk from the buyer to the bank.

Chapter 6

Cash Flow Analysis and Forecasting

In earlier chapters, we stated that financial analysis is the starting point of credit analysis. This chapter illustrates how financial analysis is used to reach observations about the credit quality of two companies – Disney and Enron.

A company's capital structure is determined by the nature of the risk of its business. Business risk is characterized by the volatility of its earnings and cash flow. If volatility is low (earnings and cash flow are stable), a company or enterprise, even an individual, can easily exist with a relatively high degree of debt (leverage). If volatility is high, due to the risk characteristics of the company and its industry, the ability to operate with a high degree of debt is limited. This is due to the risk that the company's cash flow would be insufficient to meet its operating needs and service its debt. Obviously, this is a situation that leads to insolvency and bankruptcy.

High liquidity can modify this risk, but negative cash flow can rapidly "eat up" a company's liquid assets. And, as was the case with Enron (2002) and Bear Stearns (2008), when the providers of liquidity (lenders, counter parties, suppliers) become severely concerned that a company will run out of cash, they tend to cut off credit, and a bankruptcy is often the result.

Companies are forced into bankruptcy for one of three reasons:
- ***They run out of cash***
- ***They fear that they will run out of cash***
- ***Their suppliers of liquidity fear that the company will run out of cash***

Wall Street Journal 29 May, 2008

"In a meeting Thursday that lasted barely 10 minutes, Chairman James Cayne for the first time publicly shared his feelings *about the demise of the investment bank that he ran for 14 years. Addressing several hundred Bear Stearns shareholders, many of them employees, he spoke of his regret about the evaporation of cash that had led to the company's fire sale to J.P. Morgan in March with the federal government playing chaperone."*

The ultimate function of credit analysis is to assess the degree to which a company is at risk of running out of cash. This entails assessing historic and future cash flow generation, and current and future liquidity.

Cash from operating activities is the key indicator of the extent to which a company has the ability to fund investments, operate, pay dividends, and repay debt, without having to resort to outside sources of financing.

Cash (and cash equivalents) from operating activities is the most important information that a credit analyst must understand. While companies that are growing rapidly might not produce enough cash from operations to fund all investments, at some point growth slows, and cash flow, after investments, must become positive.

Companies cannot sustain negative cash flow from operations, and after investments, for indefinite periods of time. This is a fundamental concept of corporate finance – if investments do not produce a return that is greater than the cost of capital (which includes debt and equity), the providers of that capital (equity and debt investors), will no longer be willing to supply capital. One of the goals of equity analysts and credit analysts (also collectively referred to as "securities analysts") is to identify the degree to which the management of a company is using its capital effectively. Ultimately this is measured as a cash return on capital, not an accounting return on capital. Dividends are paid, and debt is reduced from cash, not from accounting earnings.

Cash Flow Analysis

Typical international accounting standards provide that companies will produce three sets of basic financial information (plus notes):

- Income Statement
- Balance Sheet
- Cash Flow Statement

The International Accounting Standards Boards (IASB) issued "IAS 7 Statement of Cash Flows" in 1992. It is the standard rule for preparing the Cash Flow Statement. According to IAS 7, companies which issue financial statements in accordance with IASB standards "must provide information about the historical changes in cash and cash equivalents of an entity by means of a statement of cash flows..."

Cash flows are inflows and outflows of cash and cash equivalents (very liquid investments) which arise during a specific accounting period from:

- operating activities
- investing activities
- financing activities

The Cash Flow Statement will reconcile and balance all uses and sources of cash to show how the cash balance changed from one period to the next.

Equity and credit analysts often use variations of the cash flow statement for certain analysis objectives. Free Cash Flow, EBIT (earnings before interest and taxes), and EBITDA (earnings before interest, taxes, depreciation and amortization) are described below within the context of the three components of the cash flow statement – operating activities, investing activities, and financing activities.

Cash from Operating Activities

The first section of a cash flow statement is intended to show the amount of cash that is generated from the company's fundamental business activity –cash revenue generation less cash expenses. Cash flow from operations is one of the most important pieces of information for both financial and credit analysis. It identifies the fundamental strength of a company to generate "cash" profits, as opposed to accounting profits.

The calculation of operating cash flow starts with a company's net income. Adjustments must then be made for "non-cash" charges to income, such as depreciation. Non-cash expenses are added to net income reflect an approximation of cash and "cash equivalents" that is generated from operations.

According to international accounting standards, cash from operating activities is shown after all non-cash and non-financing changes in working capital. In other words, changes in the non-cash components of current assets and current liabilities, which include accounts receivable (from customers), inventories, pre-paid assets, accounts payable (to suppliers) and other payables.

A net increase in working capital is considered a use of cash from operations – current assets would have increased more than current liabilities. A decrease in net working capital implies the generation of cash – current liabilities would have grown more than current assets, or current assets declined more than current liabilities.

The inclusion of the net change in working capital in the cash flow statement is the accepted accounting standard. However, for the purposes of credit analysis, it is useful to separately analyze cash from operations from cash used or generated by changes in working capital. This is due to the fact that some forms of current liabilities are equivalent to debt, but difficult for an analyst to identify. Therefore it is useful to look at cash from operations before and after the impact of changes in working capital. This will be illustrated in the two examples later in the lesson.

The first section of a company's statement of cash flows concludes with:

Net Cash Provided by Operating Activities = Net Income + Depreciation and Amortization – Changes in Working Capital

EBIT, earnings before interest and taxes, is used by financial analysts to examine the basic earnings and cash generating history of a company, before the consideration of how it is financed or taxed. Examining the historic trend in EBIT provides a basic indication of a company's business and cash flow volatility or stability. When compared to the capital base, it provides a basic ratio about indication of the degree to which a company has the capability of producing a competitive return on capital, before interest and taxes.

However, like death, taxes cannot be avoided. Nor can interest expense be ignored. EBIT is therefore an insufficient indicator of a company's true ability to generate cash for investing and return to the owners.

EBITDA, earnings before interest, taxes, depreciation and amortization, is a popular, if somewhat misleading metric of a company's fundamental cash producing capability. It is used extensively by credit analysts to identify a company's debt capacity in leveraged buyouts – transactions where companies are purchased using very high amounts of debt. These are also referred to as "HLT's" or "highly leveraged transactions. EBITDA is used as a starting point to determine how much debt a company can service – both interest and principal. It ignores two extremely important uses of cash that cannot be ignored if a company or enterprise is to grow and remain viable – working capital and capital expenditures. It EBITDA is used to predict cash available for debt service, an analyst estimate what will be required every year for working capital and at least a minimum amount of capital expenditures for regular maintenance.

Cash Used for Investing Activities

All companies must make capital expenditures of some sort to sustain their business, whether for maintenance or for growth. Some investments are postpone able, but a certain amount of investment must be made periodically in order to maintain revenue and service customers.

Acquisitions of businesses are also included in this category of cash expenditures.

As noted above, if companies do not produce returns on investments that are greater than their cost of capital (cost of equity and cost of debt), they will not produce value nor sufficient cash to pay interest, reduce debt, or return capital to owners in the form of dividends.

Successful investments should return sufficient cash to "pay back" the investment with a return that covers the cost of the investment, the cost of interest to fund the investment, and a positive return to the owners of the equity. The purpose of investing is to maintain cash flow and to increase cash flow via new sources of revenue. This must be done while producing a positive return on invested capital. A risk adjusted interest rate for debt investors, and a risk adjusted return on equity for equity investors.

For high performing companies, cash flow from operations is often sufficient to fund all investing activities.

For companies that are not producing high returns on capital, and for high growth companies, cash flow from operations often is not sufficient to fund all capital expenditures and other investments. These companies must resort to external sources for funding. But, unless a company has tremendous prospects for future growth and profitability (positive cash flow), and can convince the suppliers of capital of that fact, it cannot run an operating cash flow deficit forever. At some point the suppliers of capital will lose confidence in a company's ability to produce positive operating cash flow.

There is one industry that has managed to continue to attract financing over long periods of poor or non-existent operating cash flow. What is it, and why?
The answer is the airline industry. The reason is the nature of the assets and the way they are financed. This is the topic of a future lesson. But, the short answer is that there are a number of lending companies that specialize in aircraft, and are willing to lend purely against the value of the aircraft, regardless of the cash flow of the airline that is utilizing the aircraft. This is an example of a "one way out" loan that was discussed in Lesson Three. In general, these loans work well and the lenders receive full payment with an acceptable return.

The second section of the statement of cash flows concludes with:

Net Cash Used in Investing Activities = Net Income + Depreciation and Amortization – Changes in Working Capital – Capital Expenditures and Investments

Free Cash Flow

This is not a phrase that will be seen on an accounting statement of cash flows. But, in effect, it is on the statement, as it is the difference between **Net Cash Provided by Operating Activities (after working capital)** and **Net Cash Used in Investing Activities**.

Free cash flow is the cash produced by a company from operations, after working capital changes, and after all capital expenditures and investments. It is the cash available to pay dividends and the principal amount of debt. It is the amount of cash that can be taken out of a company while ensuring that there have been sufficient expenditures on operations and continuing investment, including working capital.

A company or enterprise that has a history of positive free cash flow has been able to "self finance" – it covers all operating expenses and capital expenditures from the revenue it generates. It will use this "free cash flow" to build liquidity, pay dividends or reduce debt.

A company's debt capacity, the amount of debt it can safely maintain and manage, is primarily a function of its historic and projected free cash flow.

If a company has negative "free cash flow", it is spending more than its operations can support; i.e., operating cash flow is not sufficient to cover all capital expenditures. In the worse situations, revenue may not even be sufficient to cover operating expenses and cash flow even before capital expenditures would be negative. It will have to finance this operating deficit with outside funds – either more debt or more equity. An historic pattern of negative cash flow is a significant danger sign which must be explained. At some point all enterprises must be able to produce positive cash flow. It's the only way that debt and equity investors can achieve a positive return on their investment.

Free cash flow is often used by equity analysts for the valuation of an enterprise. Using the discounted cash flow method of valuation, the value of an enterprise is the present value of future free cash flow, discounted at an appropriate cost of capital. Most assets are valued in this manner, including real estate and fixed income instruments such as bonds. The value of a bond is the present value of the future payments. The value of an office building is the present value of its future free cash flow, which is the total of future rents, less all cash expenses, including interest, taxes, operating expenses, and capital expenditures.

The technique for establishing the value of a company and an office building is basically the same. It's the calculation of the present value of a stream of future cash payments to the owner of the company or the building.

The difference between establishing the value of these two types of business enterprises, an operating company and a real estate venture, rests in the challenge of predicting the future free cash flow. The future fee cash flow of a company is generally hard to estimate. It requires extensive knowledge of products, competition, expenses, and industry dynamics, including innovation and technological change. An equity analyst will use this information to establish value. A credit analyst will use this information to establish debt capacity and credit quality.

The future free cash flow produced by an office building may, or may not, be easier to forecast than that for a business enterprise. This depends upon the nature of the leases for the space in a building. If the building does not have major tenants with long term leases, the value is based on estimates of rents and occupancy rates. This is subject to many risks and potential volatility – location, market rents, the local real estate market, the local economic situation, etc.

On the other hand, if the office building had only one tenant with a long term master lease, the future cash flow, and the value of the building, is easy to establish. With a master lease the tenant is responsible for all building operating costs. The risk of the cash flow rests on the credit risk of the tenant. If it is a large, and highly credit worthy entity, the value of the building is the present value of the rents to be paid over the term of the lease, plus the present value of the estimated market value of the building at the time of the termination of the lease. Estimating the terminal value of an asset at a distant time is not an easy task. But if it is much more than 10 years in the future, the present value is fairly small compared to the present value of the rental stream.

Forecasting Future Free Cash Flow

The primary role of the credit analyst and equity analyst is to make predictions about the future free cash flow of an enterprise. The equity analyst does this to establish a view about market value. The credit analyst does this to determine debt capacity, and to identify the degree to which the current level of debt, whether short term or long term, is high or low.

The task of forecasting free cash flow is not an easy one for most companies. The process starts with the principles of Lesson I – understanding the dynamics of a company's industry, its competitive position, and the model of how it produces, or hopes to produce, an adequate return on capital (equity) that is sustainable. A significant component of this process is making a judgment about the capabilities, competence, and credibility of the managers of the enterprise. This was succinctly stated by the famous financier, J.P. Morgan...

"Lending is not based primarily on money or property. No sir, the first thing is character"

Financing Activities

The final part of the cash flow statement shows changes in sources of financing, both debt and equity, and the reconciliation of the change in cash. If cash flow after investments is positive (positive free cash flow), this section will show how the cash generated is deployed – net reduction in debt, dividends or repurchase of capital stock, or a net increase in cash and cash equivalents. If cash flow after investments is negative, this section will show how the deficit was financed – debt, equity, or a net reduction in cash and cash equivalents.

This third section of the statement of cash flows concludes with:

Net Cash Provided by Financing Activities and, the reconciliation of the change in cash from the beginning of the reporting period to the end of the reporting period:

Increase (Decrease) in cash and cash equivalents =

Net Cash Provided by Operating Activities (after change in working capital)

- **Net Cash Used in Investing Activities**

+/- Net Cash Provided by Financing Activities

The Increase (Decrease) in cash and cash equivalents from the Cash Flow Statement will be equal to:

Cash and Cash Equivalents, Beginning of period - Cash and Cash Equivalents, End of period

Two Examples of Using Historic Cash Flow Statements to Predict Future Free Cash Flow – Disney Enterprises and Enron Corporation

I. Disney Enterprises, 2001 – 2003

Disney is a large, global, diversified entertainment company.

For fiscal year 2003, Disney had:

Revenue of US$ 27 billion,

EBIT of US$ 2.8 billion,

Net income of US$1.3 billion.
EBITDA was US$4.2 billion.
Total assets of about $50 billion
Equity of about $24 billion.

The three year period of 2001 through 2003 was one of stable revenue and stable operating profitability. 2001 net income was negative due to a large restructuring charge related to dis-continued operations.

Disney is a large, profitable, company, with a substantial amount of gross cash flow (before capital expenditures), and a capital structure with moderate leverage. But this information doesn't indicate whether or not the amount of profit generated is high or low relative to the capital employed. It also does not indicate whether or not its cash flow is sufficient to fund all of its investment needs. It doesn't provide much information about the credit quality of the company.

Disney's Return on Equity was actually relatively low throughout this period. Only in the range of 5%. High performing companies will produce ROE in the range of 10% to 20%. Using the model described in Lessons I and II, Disney produced this ROE in 2003 as follows:

2003 Return on Equity (Net Income / Equity)
  $1,267 (Net Income) / $23,791 (year end equity) = 5.33%

It was 5.27% in 2002 and negative in 2001

2003 Profit Margin (Net Income / Revenue)
  $1,267 (Net Income) / $27,061 (Revenue) = 4.68%

It was 4.9% in 2002 and negative in 2001

2003 Asset Productivity (Revenue / Assets)
  $27,061 (Revenue) / $49,988 (Assets) = 54.13%

50.6 % in 2002 and 49% in 2001

2003 Leverage (Assets / Equity)
  $49,988 (Assets) / $23,791 (Equity) = 210%

51% in 2002 and 49% in 2001

2003 ROE = Profit Margin X Asset Productivity X Leverage

2003 ROE = 4.68% (Profit Margin) X 54.1% (Asset Prod) X 2.101 (Leverage)
 = 5.33%

5.3% in 2002 and negative in 2001

Negative net income in 2001 was an aberration as revenue and operating profit before the special charge were consistent with the subsequent years. The company took a very large "non cash" restructuring charge.

Based on the information from this model, it would appear that If Disney were to improve return on equity in years subsequent to 2003, it probably would focus on profit margins and asset productivity. In 2003, its very large asset base of US$50 billion produced revenue of US$27 billion. It apparently is making large investments that are not producing significant revenue. It was also dealing with fairly low profit margins, which might not be logically intuitive in a business where a "blockbuster" movie could produce very big returns.

Disney's operating cash flow during this period was consistent and positive before any impact of changes in working capital…

CONSOLIDATED STATEMENTS OF CASH FLOWS

US$ million	2003	2002	2001
Net Income	1267	1236	-158
Non-cash adjustments to net income			
Depreciation	1059	1021	987
Amortization of Intangible Assets	18	21	767
Other non-cash items (expense and income)	293	35	1697

CASH FROM OPERATING ACTIVITY

	2637	2313	3293

Even in 2001, when net income was negative, operating cash flow was not only positive, but higher than in the two subsequent years. The cause of the 2001 loss was a large restructuring charge which represented an accounting charge, not an immediate cash loss.

EBITDA is an even larger amount, since Disney is a large taxpayer. $4219 in 2003. But, this is one of the reasons why EBITDA is not a good proxy for cash flow for profitable companies – taxes and interest must be paid!

EBITDA - Earnings Before Interest, Taxes, Depreciation   and Amortization

	4219	3619	4769

Changes in working capital were a positive contributor to cash flow, but not in any significant amounts....

CHANGES IN WORKING CAPITAL

Accounts Receivable	-194
Inventory	-6
Other current assets	-28
Accounts Payable	275
Other current liabilities	217
Cash from changes in Working Capital	264

CASH FROM OPERATIONS AND WORKING CAPITAL   **2901**

As described earlier, the primary function of cash flow analysis is to identify the degree to which an enterprise is able to fund its ongoing investments and capital expenditures from operations. Disney has a consistent history of generating sufficient cash from operations to fund most of its investments.....

CASH USED FOR INVESTMENTS

	2003
Investments in Property and Equipment	1049
Acquistions	-130
Divestitures	166
Sale of investments	40
Investments	-14
Other	-47

NET CASH INVESTMENTS   -1034

CASH FLOW AFTER INVESTMENTS   1867

In the three year period of 2001 – 2003, Disney produced positive **FREE CASH FLOW** of $2.010 billion!

What did it do with this Free Cash Flow?

FINANCING

Borrowed Money	1635
Repayment of Borrowed Money	-2059
Dividends	-429
Other	-670
NET CASH FROM FINANCING	**-1523**
CHANGE IN CASH	**344**
Cash and Cash Equivalents Beginning of Year	**1,239**
Cash and Cash Equivalents End of Year	**1,583**
Change in Cash and Cash Equivalents	**344**

The final section of the Disney 2003 Statement of Cash Flow shows that liquidity increased, with the cash and cash equivalent balance increasing by $344 million. The company used the remainder of its excess cash to reduce debt by about $400 million, pay dividends of $429 million, which seems to be a consistent dividend payout program, and it bought back stock of about $670 million.

At the end of fiscal year 2003, Disney had had total outstanding debt of approximately US$ 13 billion. Does this seem to be reasonable?

Depending upon the analyst's view of the future performance of Disney, the answer is probably "yes".

A company's ability to maintain a certain level of debt is primarily a function of the nature of the riskiness of its business and industry, and its consequent cash flow volatility. Disney is a very large, well established business, with relatively stable revenue and cash flow, and a history of performance. In the three years through 2003, it produced Free Cash Flow of $2 billion.

If there is a reasonable judgment that Disney can continue to produce free cash flow in this range, then total debt of about $13 billion could be amortized in six years. Of course, if the company is doing well, there is no reason to pay off all debt, nor would the company wish to suspend its dividend. The fact that the debt can be repaid or refinanced creates a high degree of confidence in the suppliers of debt.

Refinancing of debt as a "way out" by itself is not an acceptable answer to a company's credit quality. The refinancing will take place only if the providers of credit believe that a company can produce positive free cash flow to amortize the debt if further refinancing becomes unavailable, for whatever reason. This is known as 'refinancing" risk.

Does the Disney entertainment business have significant business risk? The answer is clearly yes. But it is the job of professional managers to work through these risks and manage them.

Standard & Poor's described the Disney strategic position and risk in a report published in May, 2008....

*"As a content-oriented company, DIS's top strategic priorities include creativity
and innovation, international expansion, and leveraging new technology applications. Under CEO Robert Iger, we see senior management aggressively exploring new avenues to offer its branded content, characters and entertainment franchises across emerging digital platforms such as broadband and wireless, while making further investments in other areas such as video games. Recent initiatives include: a deal to provide content from its ABC networks and the film studios on Apple's video iPod, the launch of Disney Mobile cellular phone service, and an ad-supported streaming of ABC's shows."*

"We have a neutral fundamental outlook on the movies and entertainment sub-industry. We believe continued gradual shifts from traditional distribution windows to newer platforms such as video-on-demand and iPods create potential challenges for entertainment content providers already vulnerable to industry saturation and rampant piracy. We are also wary of potential disruptions after the recent writers' strike. However, we see content providers starting to reinvent business models to capitalize on a nascent digital market, which will likely expand rapidly and generate increasingly meaningful contributions to revenue in the years ahead."

Disney is in a very dynamic and challenging industry, and it has been managed relatively well. Subsequent to 2003, Disney's operating performance has improved steadily, due largely to improved profit margins. Revenue growth has been moderate, but net income has grown substantially since 2003, as has Return on Equity, which was 14.9% in 2007. Free Cash Flow has grown to $6 billion.

Income Statement (Million $)

	2007	2006	2005	2004
Revenue	35,510	34,285	31,944	30,752
Operating Income	8,272	6,914	5,446	5,258
Net Income	4,674	3,374	2,569	2,345

Balance Sheet & Other Financial Data (Million $)

	2007	2006	2005	2004
Cash	3,670	2,411	1,723	2,042
Total Assets	60,928	59,998	53,158	53,902
Common Equity	30,753	31,820	26,210	26,081
Capital Exp	1,566	1,299	1,823	1,427
Cash Flow	6,165	4,810	3,908	3,555
% Net Income of Revenue	13.1	9.8	8.0	7.6
% Return on Equity	14.9	11.6	9.8	9.4

Any extensive credit analysis of Disney would review the risks, operations, and future prospects of its various key businesses. But a quick review of historic cash flow and operations, along with an assessment of the appropriateness of its capital structure, provides a basic assessment of the credit risk of an enterprise. It's easy to make a preliminary determination that Disney's debt level relative to its cash flow is moderate, and that the credit risk of Disney is low.

The next example shows a very different situation – Enron in 2000, just prior to its surprise bankruptcy and liquidation.

II. Enron Corporation, 1998 through 2000

The epic of Enron's extraordinary risk and fall has been well documented in a book and movie of the same title "The Smartest Guys in the Room". The former Chairman and CEO of Enron were convicted of criminal fraud and sentenced to prison. Enron's bankers have been sued for complicity in the fraud, which was presumably designed to overstate Enron's performance, and its financial position. In the years just prior to its demise, analysts were almost universal in their praise of the company's performance and its prospects. In retrospect, many of the analysts did not understand how the company made money, nor the degree to which it was taking very high business risks.

A review of Enron's cash flow prior to 2001 indicates that analysts should have been much more skeptical about the company's financial stability and future. Enron consistently did not produce sufficient operating cash flow to fund its investments. It's Free Cash Flow was consistently negative.

During the 1990's, Enron transformed itself from an oil and gas pipeline company into a trading company. Gross revenue skyrocketed from US$13 billion in 1996 to US$100 billion in 2000. This is a growth rate that is hard to fathom, let alone manage.

In reality, much of the growth was due to trading activity, and, for credit analysis, it's more appropriate to look at net revenue, after the cost of merchandise that is traded. This is analogous to the reporting of revenue for most financial institutions, which is net of interest expense. Gross revenue is misleading, because, for a bank, it is primarily a function of interest rate levels. The better measure is the "net spread" – revenue after cost of funds. In retrospect, Enron was more like a bank than an energy company.

In a review of the Enron fiasco well after the fact, a senior manager of Moody's, in a private interview with the author, stated that "if we had reviewed Enron in our Financial Institutions group, rather than in our Energy group, we might better have identified the problem".

For Enron, revenue after "cost of traded merchandise" shows a very different situation. Net revenue growth was substantial, but actual net revenue was very small relative to gross revenue, and income was also small relative to gross revenue and the size of the assets employed.

From the standpoint of cash flow, Enron was investing in excess of its operating cash flow in every single year since before 1996. This should have been a warning for every analyst who was judging the risks and credit quality of the company.

	2000	1999	1998	1997
(millions)				
Total Revenue	**100.8**	**40.1**	**31.3**	**20.3**
Cost of Production	94.5	34.8	26.4	17.3
Net Revenue	6.3	5.4	4.9	3.0
Net Revenue/ Total Rev	6.2%	13.3%	15.6%	14.6%
Operating Expense	4.3	4.5	3.5	2.9
Operating Income	2.0	0.9	1.4	0.1
Net Other Income	0.5	1.2	0.2	0.6

EBIT	2.5	2.1	1.6	0.7
Net Income (after tax and interest)	1.0	0.9	0.7	0.1
Profit Margin (net income / Net Revenue)	15.6%	16.7%	14.4%	3.5%
Asset Productivity (Revenue / Total Assets)	9.6%	16.0%	16.1%	13.1%

Enron's profitability was not very high, as measured by Return on Equity, but its leverage was very high. Return on equity was never more than 10%, and leverage was steadily increasing. At the end of 2000, Assets were 5.7 times equity (equity was less than 20% of total assets). Debt was increasing at a substantial rate, while profitability was stable, and free cash flow was negative. In each year, capital expenditures exceeded the generation of cash from operations.

Over this four year time period, Enron's ROE of about 10%, was produced by the use of high leverage, moderate profit margins, and very low asset productivity. At the end of year 2000, Enron had total assets of about US$65 billion, and this produced net revenue of only $6.3 billion. With what seem to be reasonable profit margins, Enron had to use high leverage to generate a mediocre ROE.

($million)	2000	1999	1998	1997
Total Assets	65,503	33,381	29,350	22,552
Total Liabilities	54.033	23,811	22.302	15,504
Net Worth	11,470	9,570	7,048	7,048
Leverage (Assets / Equity)	571%	348%	416%	320%
Return on Equity (ROE)	8.54%	9.33%	9.97%	1.47%
Cash from Operations	3,000	2,228	1,873	276

Capital Expenditures	3,314	3,085	3,564	2,092

Even before examining the Statement of Cash flow for Enron, the basic situation by 2000 should have raised a certain degree of skepticism about the nature of Enron's capital structure relative to the volatility of its cash flow. The company was growing very rapidly in a business (energy trading) that, by definition, is very risky. It's reported profitability was moderate, at best, and its leverage was increasing dramatically.

A simple cash flow analysis showed a situation that was even more serious. At first glance, Enron seemed to be producing substantial increases in cash flow from operations. The situation changes significantly if the change in working capital is extracted from cash from operations.

Prior to the year 2000, working capital used cash as the company expanded. Working capital was a use of cash, as is usually the situation in a growing company.

In the year 2000, as trading activities expanded exponentially, working capital became a source of cash. While the explanation is not obvious, it is reasonable to question the very large decline in inventory levels, and it is probable that the increase in current liabilities was an indirect form of short term debt.

	2000	1999	1998	1997
Cash from Operations	3,000	2,228	1,873	276
EBITDA	4,513	3,330	2,752	736
Cash from change in Working capital	1,769	(1000)	(233)	(65)
Cash from Operations and Change in Working Capital	4,779	1,228	1,640	211

The extremely large increase in cash from operations and working capital is unusual. It would be prudent for a credit analyst to assume that it was not sustainable. If Enron's business continued as it had been, it would not be unreasonable to assume that it could produce cash from operations in the range of $1.5 billion to $2.0 billion on a sustainable basis. But even this assumption is risky, as the nature of Enron's business was becoming increasingly risky and volatile.

Enron's need for cash to fund its investing activities was substantial, and growing every year. In 2000, it's cash flow after investments was positive at $515 million. In the 3 years prior to that, it was negative each year by close to $2 billion.

	2000	1999	1998	1997
Net Cash Investments	(4,264)	(3,607)	(3,965)	(2,146)
Cash Flow after Investments	515	(2,279)	(2,325)	(1,935)

In the year 2000, Enron did have positive cash flow after investments, including the change in working capital. If the working capital contribution was actually a form of hidden debt, then it was still continuing a long pattern of investing more than it was producing from operations.

Enron funded its cash flow deficit with a combination of debt and equity.

The company also seemed to maintain an extraordinarily low level of cash compared to the rapidly growing size of its balance sheet. At the end of 2000, it had cash and cash equivalents of $1.374 billion, compared to total assets of $65.5 billion.

One of the key factors of success for a trading company is liquidity and market confidence. Enron not only did not maintain much liquidity, it also managed to fund much of its trading activity through special purpose subsidiary companies where the debt did not appear on its balance sheet. In effect, Enron was operating with much greater leverage than was shown on the financial statements.

When the suppliers of short term credit to Enron finally realized that they did not fully understand how the company was generating its revenue, and funding its activities, they suspended credit availability. This led to the rapid demise and bankruptcy of the company. But, as illustrated here, these suppliers of credit should have been very skeptical of a company that was consistently investing more cash than it generated from its operating activities. At the end, the suppliers of credit to Enron were clearly not convinced that these investments would generate sufficient cash in the future to amortize all of Enron's outstanding debt.

"Companies go bankrupt for three reasons....
They run out of cash
They fear that they will run out of cash
Their suppliers of credit fear that they will run out of cash"

Debt Capacity and Future Free Cash Flow

The performance benchmark that should be monitored by corporate CEO's and boards of directors, as well as equity and credit analysts, is a simple one – cash generation. Cash generated by the operations of the enterprise is what is returned to investors, both debt and equity. The ability to generate cash from operations, after the need to invest in working capital and capital expenditures, is the ultimate source of providing the desired returns to equity and debt investors. While the sale of assets, or the entire company, might produce the desired return, the sale will take place only if the assets or company have value.

Ultimately, all value rests in the present value of future cash flows.

There are periods of time where investment opportunities (acquisitions and capital expenditures) will exceed the ability of an enterprise to fund them entirely from internally generated cash flow. But eventually, these investments must produce a positive return in order to repay the debt or to produce a positive return on the capital used to make the investments.

The market value of an enterprise is the present value of its future free cash flow. A smart CEO will focus on the underlying factor of the market value of an enterprise – cash flow. He or she will miss fundamental factors if the only focus is on the market value of the company in the form of the price of the stock. The focus must be on generating Free Cash Flow. By doing so, they will maximize the value of the enterprise - the present value of future free cash flow.

A good CEO or business owner will also understand the risks of using debt in the capital structure, and the fact that there is a limit to the amount of debt that can be employed. This limit is determined by the amount of free cash flow that will be available in the future, with a high degree of confidence, to service debt.

If free cash flow is negative, and financing is required to maintain a certain level of liquidity (cash and cash equivalents), the managers of an enterprise will have to find a source to provide this financing. More often than not, they will approach a lending institution (bank). Over time they may try to raise debt or equity from capital market sources is that option is available to them. The ability to raise external sources of funding, debt or equity, is dependent upon the managers' ability to adequately, and credibly, explain a strategy for the business that will show how it will produce future free cash flow.

How does a bank credit analyst or lending officer respond to a request to fund a free cash flow deficit? What does the credit analyst or lender do when the company asks for a loan?

The equity and credit analyst role is to assess and judge whether or not the company's strategy makes sense. This will be done in the context of the industry model, competitive factors, quality of management, adequacy of the capital structure, and the macro-economic environment.

This brings us back to the fundamental questions of the extension of credit that were covered in previous lessons. What's the purpose and how will it be repaid?

"Lending is not based primarily on money or property. No sir, the first thing is character" – J.P. Morgan

The goal of credit analysis is to make a judgment about an obligor's ability and willingness to pay back what it owes, when it is owed. This means that the analyst must understand all of the issues raised by Mr. Morgan – money, property, and character.

Chapter 7

The Process of Credit Analysis - Making Credit Decisions

Debt Capacity and Cash Flow

The capital structure of a business (the combination of debt and equity on the balance sheet) should be designed to match the operating risks of the business. Business risk is characterized by the volatility of revenue, expenses and cash flow. If volatility is low, and free cash flow is positive, a business enterprise, or even an individual, can easily exist with a relatively high degree of debt (leverage).

If volatility is high, due to the risk characteristics of the company and its industry, the ability to operate with a high degree of debt is limited. This is due to the risk that the company's cash flow would be insufficient to meet its operating needs and service its debt. If a company cannot produce enough cash to service debt after its operating expenses, it will eventually become insolvent and bankrupt.

The amount of debt a business (or individual) can maintain is a function of its free cash flow – the amount of cash after all necessary expenses that, including capital expenditure and investments, is available to service debt.

Cash from operating activities is the key indicator of the extent to which a company has the ability to fund investments, operate, pay dividends, and repay debt, without having to resort to outside sources of financing.

Accounting profits are not the same as cash!

The ultimate function of credit analysis is to assess the degree to which a business, or any type of enterprise, is at risk of running out of cash, or sources of cash, both in the short term and in the long term.

The result of this assessment is often articulated in the form of a **risk rating** or **debt rating**. Bankers will be risk rating most obligors and credit facility, in accordance with modern portfolio management and the standards of Basel II bank capital regulations. Debt ratings are issued by rating agencies, but many investment bankers will estimate debt ratings for a variety of fund raising purposes. The concept of portfolio management and risk ratings is the subject of Lesson VII. A risk rating is a quantitative indicator of the probability of default of a payment obligation.

The three fundamental steps of the credit analysis process are:

1) Assessing the cash flow generating opportunity of an enterprise, and its industry, and the stability or volatility of the future revenue, expenses, and free cash flow. This requires an understanding of how an enterprise produces an acceptable return on capital – the combination of profit margin, asset turnover, and leverage. It also requires an assessment of management – its strategy, competence and track record both in absolute terms and relative to its competitors.

2) Analyzing and assessing historic and current liquidity, and

3) Analyzing historic and forecasting future net cash flow generation with the goal of assessing debt capacity – whether or not the level of debt is high, moderate, or low relative to future net cash flow.

Cash generated from operating activities is the most important information that a credit analyst must understand. Accounting profits are not the same as cash generated from operations!

Free cash flow is the cash produced by a company from operations, after working capital changes, and after all capital expenditures and investments. It is the cash available to pay dividends and the principal amount of debt. It is the amount of cash that can be taken out of a company while ensuring that there have been sufficient expenditures on operations and continuing investment, including working capital.

A company or enterprise that has a history of positive free cash flow has been able to "self finance" – it covers all operating expenses and capital expenditures from the revenue it generates. It will use this "free cash flow" to build liquidity, pay dividends or reduce debt.

Companies that are growing rapidly usually do not produce enough cash from operations to fund all investments - the cash flow deficit will be funded from outside sources – debt or equity. But, at some point growth slows, and cash flow, after investments, must become positive. Otherwise investors will not have a reasonable prospect of obtaining a return on their investment.

Enron's bankruptcy was partially the result of investors losing confidence that the investments that they were funding would eventually produce a positive return. Investors, both institutional investors and bank lenders, stopped supplying funds when they began to question whether or not Enron was really profitable, or had the capability of becoming more profitable in the future. They finally focused on cash generation, not accounting profit.

A company's debt capacity, the amount of debt it can safely maintain and manage, is primarily a function of its historic and projected free cash flow.

The Credit Decision Process, and Cash Flow Forecasting: Short Term Lending and Long Term Lending

Both credit analysts and equity analysts must make predictions about the future free cash flow of an enterprise. The equity analyst does this to establish an estimate about the market value of an enterprise. Market value, by definition, is the present value of future free cash flow generated by an enterprise.

The credit analyst tires to predict future free cash flow to determine debt capacity, and to identify the degree to which the current level of debt, whether short term or long term, is high or low. The potential volatility of future cash flow, and the amount of debt relative to that cash flow, is the basis for establishing both debt ratings (public debt or equivalent) and risk ratings (bank debt and other credit obligations). So, the analyst is not only predicting the amount of future cash flow, he or she is also assessing the volatility of that future cash flow prediction – a range for the expected amount of future cash flow. If the amount of debt relative to future cash flow is high, there will be a higher probability of default. This probability will be modified by the degree of expected volatility of the future cash flow. If the volatility is low (very stable cash flow), even a highly levered enterprise might have a good debt rating. If volatility is high, a company with even a small amount of debt might still have a poor debt rating, due to the higher risk of default arising from very unstable cash flow.

The task of forecasting free cash flow is not an easy one for either companies or analysts. The process starts with the principles of understanding the dynamics of a company's industry, its competitive position, prospects for growth, and the model of how it produces, or hopes to produce, an adequate return on capital (equity), that is sustainable.

The equity and credit analyst role is to assess and judge whether or not the company's strategy makes sense. This will be done in the context of the industry model, competitive factors, quality of management, adequacy of the capital structure, and the macro economic environment. It is a judgment about how a company makes money (produces real cash), and an assessment about the risk associated with its plan to make money in the future. Making money is about producing cash, not accounting profit.

This brings us back to the fundamental questions of the extension of credit that were covered in previous chapters.

"What's the purpose of the extension of credit, and how will it be repaid?"

"Lending is not based primarily on money or property. No sir, the first thing is character" – J.P. Morgan

The goal of credit analysis is to make a judgment about an obligor's ability and willingness to pay back what it owes, when it is owed. This means that the analyst must understand all of the issues raised by Mr. Morgan – money, property, and character.

In one of the previous chapters, we stated an old banking aphorism: **"Never lend short, where you wouldn't lend long"**

This is a statement that is invariably confusing to an inexperienced banker or credit analyst. But, the meaning is straight forward. It describes the principle that if a borrower can't pay back a short term loan, for whatever reason, it becomes a long term loan, and the lender will have to be paid back from operating cash flow in the future.

If a business with very little excess liquidity has a short term cash problem which prevents it from fulfilling its short term obligations, supplier of short term credit to that business will probably not be repaid in accordance with their terms and expectations. They will become long term creditors – they will have to renegotiate their terms of payment. Therefore, even short term creditors must have confidence that the prospects for the generation of long term excess cash flow are good. If there is a liquidity squeeze, the creditor will have to be repaid from cash flow from operations over time.

While all loans are repaid from cash, it is obviously more difficult to predict cash flow over time than it is in the near term. If a banker is not confident about a borrower's cash flow in the distant future, he or she shouldn't lend at all, no matter how short the loan. Short term loans to weak borrowers have a tendency to not get paid!

In situations where the lender is not willing to take a risk that the obligor can't generate the cash to pay back on obligation, or the risk that it won't be willing to pay back an obligation, there is still a time honored means of extending credit. By taking excellent collateral, that can be liquidated quickly and for an amount that will be sufficient to repay the obligation.

So, the phrase "never lend short where you wouldn't lend long" means that a good banker or analyst must assess the long term cash flow of a borrower, regardless of the nominal length of the proposed or requested loan.

Nevertheless, once a lender decides that an obligor is worth having as a client or as an investment, assessing short term cash needs in response to a request for a short term loan must be done, and it is not necessarily an easy process.

Short Term Lending – Liquidity Analysis and Forecasting

All credit obligations are paid from cash – cash from existing liquidity, cash generated from the sale or liquidation of assets, or cash generated over time from the operations of a business.

Working capital and liquidity analysis and forecasting are fundamental to the cash planning process for all enterprises.

Small agricultural enterprises have a straightforward, seasonal, need for working capital. Cash is expended in the spring to plant a crop, and during the growing season to tend the growth. It is collected at the harvest. If a farmer borrows money in the spring to finance a crop, the presumption generally would be that the loan would be repaid from cash generated by the harvest.

A distributor of consumer or industrial products might borrow to finance a seasonal build up of inventory, or a seasonal peak in accounts receivable, with the proceeds of the sale of the merchandise and collection of the receivables used to repay any short term financings.

Manufacturers potentially have a more complicated working capital situation, as the time between the need for cash and the receipt of cash can be relatively long. Raw materials must be acquired, products produced, final inventory distributed, and accounts receivable collected.

In all of these cases, a well run enterprise will try to estimate the amount of cash that will be used and generated during this period – the crop cycle, the inventory cycle, or the inventory/manufacturing/collection cycle. They will forecast their cash needs and cash generation over a period of six to twelve months, or even longer. This is basic business planning which should be done by all companies. It is basic working capital management, and will result in an estimate of how much cash a company will need to maintain to fund its working capital requirements during its periodic "**operating cycle**".

A business operating cycle is the process by which products are either created or acquired, sold, and cash is collected. This is sometimes referred to as the **cash conversion cycle**.

The cash conversion cycle is the period from the initiation of the production or acquisition of goods, through the collection of payment from customers. This period is going to be much longer for manufacturers than it would be for wholesalers or distributors. And, it will vary significantly for manufacturers of different types of products.

For retailers, the cycle is relatively simple. Goods are purchased, either for cash or credit, and sold, either for cash or credit. The business model of a discount retailer (for example, Wal*Mart) depends upon high degrees of inventory turnover and cash sales. Merchandise is purchased, warehoused, and distributed to stores in as short a time as possible. This can readily be calculated as "days' inventory" – the average amount of time that inventory is held.

For example, in 2007 the total cost of goods sold by **Wal-Mart** was $286.5 billion. Inventory at the end of 2007 was $35.2 billion, and it was $33.7 billion at the end of 2006, for average inventory of $34.5 billion. Dividing COGS by average inventory, we get 8.3. That was Wal-Mart's inventory turnover for the period, showing us that essentially, the company filled and sold everything on its shelves about eight times during the year. That is the equivalent turning over its entire inventory in 44 days ("days' inventory"). Wal-Mart needed to buy about $34 billion of inventory and hold it, on average, for 44 days before it sold it to customers and received cash. If Wal-Mart receives payment terms from its suppliers and doesn't have to pay them for 44 days, then it will not need any other source of working capital. This "**trade credit**" will be sufficient to allow Wal-Mart time to acquire, distribute, and sell its inventory. Of course, most suppliers do not give this much credit to retail distributors, even a company as powerful as Wal-Mart. Retailers must have other means of funding the purchase and warehousing of inventory. It will either be cash reserves, or other forms of financing.

For retailers, the cash cycle is relatively short – 30 to 60 days. The cash forecasting process for these companies is complex, but straightforward. They must estimate inventory purchases, payment terms, and sales.

One of the traditions of short term or seasonal lending is to enforce a "clean up" of a line of credit, which means that at some point during a cycle the loan balance will be reduced to zero. The concept was that if an enterprise was truly borrowing for short term, seasonal needs, it would generate sufficient cash at some point during the yearly cash cycle to have enough cash to pay back all short term loans. If it could not, the loans were clearly financing longer term needs, and the lender would then have to decide if the long term cash flow of the company was sufficient to repay the "non-seasonal" portion of the debt. This is a tradition that seems to have faded from common use, though it is not an unreasonable practice. The more common situation is the one in the example above, where a lender and a borrower agree upon a cash flow forecast and monitor results against that forecast.

A common approach to inventory and receivables lending is the establishment of a "borrowing base" formula where a certain percent of the value of inventory and accounts receivable will be available for loans at all times. In these situations, a borrower might be able to work with relatively high leverage, but it is based upon hard assets (inventory and receivables), and the proceeds of cash payments from customers goes to directly reduce the amount of loan outstanding in the same proportion as the borrowing base.

Forecasting the working capital needs of manufacturing enterprises is much more challenging than for retailers. They must plan purchases of raw materials, the manufacturing time of work in process, levels of inventory to meet customer demand, and collection periods. This cash cycle could be months, or even years, depending upon the product. For large capital goods, such as aircraft, it could be three years or more.

Long Term Lending – Forecasting Free Cash Flow and Debt Capacity

The goal of credit analysis is to assess the degree of risk associated with the ability (and willingness) of an enterprise to repay an obligation, in accordance with its terms. The primary role of both credit analysts and equity analysts is to make predictions about the future free cash flow of an enterprise, including an assessment of the volatility, or risk, of the future cash flow prediction.

The equity analyst does this to establish a view about market value. The credit analyst does this to determine debt capacity, and to identify the degree to which the current level of debt is high, low, or acceptable. The credit analyst must make a judgment about the amount of debt relative to the ability to service the debt in the future. Forecasting is the process of predicting cash flow and it's variance over time.

Business models vary from industry to industry, and capital structure follows the business model. Not every business can make a profit with the same capital structure, and not every business can survive with lots of financial risk in the form of high leverage.

One of the most important, and widely ignored, lessons of corporate finance is that businesses that have high operating risk are not likely to survive if they have a capital structure with high financial risk – that is, high leverage. Highly leveraged companies can survive in the long term only if their industry is not subject to a lot of volatility. There are not many industries that have this characteristic. Commercial banking is, supposedly one of these – they operate continually with high balance sheet leverage (equity is about 8% of total assets). But this is primarily due to the very liquid nature of their assets. The events of 2007 and 2008 have made it clear that many banks made very large investments in financial assets that were not liquid, and highly volatile. Of course, these were sub prime mortgages, and securitization pools of sub prime mortgages.

Even companies with high risk business models (a lot of volatility) can survive for a long time if they have "patient capital" – capital that does not have a specific maturity date. Of course, the primary form of capital that does not mature is equity. History has shown that poorly managed companies that are very well capitalized (have very little debt), can die a very slow death!

As opposed to equity, all debt matures at some point! Either by contractual agreement or by virtue of the fact that at some point market events cause lenders to withdraw their willingness to lend. This is one of the key lessons of the 2008 credit crisis. Lenders are rarely paid a sufficient return that makes them willing to accept more than a moderate level of principal risk. At some point, they want to have a return of capital. Many investors are willing to lend only if they know that they can redeem their principal (or a portion of their principal upon very short notice via a sale into a liquid market.

In a previous chapter, we explored the free cash flow generation history of Enron and Disney. The analysis showed that Enron was operating with significant cash flow deficits, while Disney was able to provide most of its cash requirements from its operating free cash flow.

Despite Enron's cash flow deficits, bankers were tripping over themselves to lend money to Enron. What was the nature of the analysis that caused Enron lenders (and rating agencies) to have confidence that the company would generate sufficient cash flow to fulfill its obligations? What was Enron's debt capacity? The Enron management team very effectively persuaded investors that the company's various investments would turn cash flow positive and provide sufficient future free cash flow to service the interest and principal of all of its debt.

Obviously, Enron's creditors accepted management's forecasts about the company's ability to grow and generate future free cash flow. They also made assumptions about its liquidity. In retrospect, at least some of these assumptions were wrong.

Enron was a trading company, which by definition is a volatile business. Yet, it had a history of building debt and operating with significant free cash flow deficits. Moreover, a lot of Enron's debt was "off balance sheet" - not totally hidden from investors, but not directly observable. In retrospect, Enron's leverage was much greater than that was assumed by many suppliers of credit and investors.

How should a banker or analyst have responded or reacted to Enron's rosy view of the future? In retrospect, with a lot of skepticism.

This takes us back to the points made throughout this book – all industries have a natural capital structure, which is a function of the business risks (operating risks) of the enterprise. Some industries operate with low cash flow volatility, some with very high volatility. Disney operates in businesses that have very high operating risk, but has done a superb job of managing these risks, largely through diversification. Disney also managed its capital structure to match the operating risks. It had a reasonable amount of debt.

Enron operated in businesses that were also very volatile. But it operated with much higher leverage than Disney, and did not offset the business risk with diversification and a conservative capital structure.

In order for an analyst to make a judgment about the adequacy of a company's capital structure, and its ability to produce enough future cash flow to service its debt, he or she must understand the strategies of each of the businesses, have complete trust and confidence in management, understand the factors that are critical to the success of each of the lines of business, and make a judgment about the company's ability to compete effectively in these businesses to achieve its cash flow goals. Needless to say, Enron's management did not provide much information for analysts to be able to do this.

What does a banker, creditor, or analyst do when confronted with a request for long term credit – a loan, a bond, a derivative, or a letter of credit?

A simple answer is to go back to the fundamental questions of credit that were outlined at the beginning of this book - Who's the borrower? What's the purpose? How will it be repaid?

Who's the Borrower is a very complex question, with significant implications. It relates to all of the issues that have been discussed so far in this course. It requires an examination of

- the nature of the company and the industry – prospects for growth, the degree of competition, the economic and regulatory environment
- the company's historic performance
- the nature and competence of management
- the company's capital structure risk relative to the business (operating) risk

The question of "Purpose" often elicits answers from a client that are confusing at best, and misleading at worst. A common response is "working capital purposes"; i.e. to fund permanent increases to fund higher levels of inventory, work in process, and receivables. But long term sources of credit might also be used for:
- capital expenditures
- operating cash deficits
- acquisitions
- investments
- derivatives for hedging – fx, interest rates, commodities
- derivatives for speculating

- letters of credit and guarantees

How will it get paid back generally presents two options – payment from cash flow, or refinancing. Assuming that an obligation is OK because it can be refinanced begs the question. It can only be refinanced if the next investor believes that he or she will be repaid. At some point, there must be a proven ability to repay or refund an obligation from excess cash flow that is generated by the enterprise.

Someone must assess the degree of risk that internally generated cash flow will be sufficient to repay all obligations when they become due. This is the role of credit analysis.

Cash flow forecasting for the long term, (and the analysis of a request for long term funding), requires the ability to forecast a number of complex issues: that result in a projection of Free Cash Flow. The elements of a long term cash flow forecast must include:

- Revenue
- Cash and non-cash expenses
- Taxes
- Interest Expense
- Working Capital
- Contingent liabilities
- Debt service
- Dividends or Distributions
- Capital Expenditure
- Investments and Acquisitions

How is long term cash flow forecasting accomplished?

First, a business is assessed according to its industry. Each industry, by virtue of its operating characteristics, the competitive environment, and the economic and geographic environment, has a set of things that must be done well in order to succeed. These are often referred to as **critical success factors.** Identifying and assessing critical success factors a fundamental aspect of strategic industry analysis and industry planning.

Second, an analyst must examine historical operating performance and cash flow. Forecasts of future operating performance and capital structure start with an understanding of historic performance and the adequacy of the existing capital structure.

Third, the analyst must determine the degree to which future cash flow is sufficient to support the capital structure of the enterprise. It would be very unusual for a business manager or CFO to try to obtain financing with a business plan that did not show adequate cash flow to service debt and meet all other obligations. The analyst must make a judgment as to whether or not the business plan that is presented makes sense. This is really a judgment about the business model and the ability of the enterprise to produce enough cash flow to service the proposed or anticipated amount of debt.   Capital Structure is the mix of debt and equity that finances the balance sheet assets.

Determining the degree of risk in the capital structure of an enterprise means making an assessment as to whether or not a business has the proper mix of debt and equity relative to its future free cash flow. Debt must be repaid at some point. Equity has no maturity.

In a previous chapter we saw an historic cash flow analysis of Disney Enterprises, Inc., through the fiscal year 2003. The following is a very basic model of how an analyst might forecast the cash flow of Disney. In this model, we take the two actual years performance of 2002 and 2003, and use it to forecasts performance for the next four years – 2004 through 2007.

While this is a mechanical exercise, it will only be valid if there is an in depth understanding of the factors that would justify the business model and Disney's ability to produce the forecasted revenue growth.

But, as a starting point, a model such as this is very useful to test basic assumptions. In this case the fundamental assumption is that revenue and expenses will grow at rates similar the growth in previous periods.

Assumptions are also made about the need to fund growth in working capital, capital expenditures, and investments.

In this forecast, the revenue growth rate is based upon the 2003 / 2002 growth rate of just under 7%. Expenses are also increased at the one year historic rate of about 6.1%. Annual interest cost of $780 million is based upon maintaining total debt about $13 billion.

Capital expenditures and investments grow each year while the amount for acquisitions is arbitrarily set between $500 million per year and $1 billion per year.

These assumptions are very arbitrary, but not unreasonable. They are at least a starting point for an analyst to try to understand the factors that will impact a company's ability to generate cash flow to service debt, while still meeting its needs for operations and expansion.

The results are comforting. If the assumptions are correct, Disney has ample debt capacity. Total debt of US$13 billion, can easily be amortized by the company's free cash flow of more than $2 billion annually. Disney has excess debt capacity. The debt rating of Disney is a function of the volatility of producing this free cash flow. This is where the analyst needs an in depth understanding of the nature of the risks of the industry, and the capability of management relative to the management of those risks.

This forecast was made solely on the basis of the 2002 and 2003 financial statements, without any examination, in retrospect, of what actually happened. The comparison between the actual results in FY 2007 and this forecast are revealing.

The forecasted total revenue, expenses and EBIT for 2007 were $35.2 billion (revenue), $31.6 billion (expenses), and $2.4 billion EBIT. The Free Cash Flow forecast was $2.4 billion.

Actual revenue in 2007 was very close to the forecast at $35.5 billion. However, the company managed to grow revenue while keeping expenses relatively flat, so that actual expenses in 2007 were $28.7 billion. There was a $1 billion gain on the sale of a business in 2007, resulting in EBIT of $8.4 billion. Actual Free Cash Flow, after dividends, was $3.8 billion, about $1.4 billion more than our forecast.

Chapter 8

Use of Credit Structure to Modify Risk
Commercial Finance and Structured Finance

"Lending is not based primarily on money or property. No sir, the first thing is character" – J.P. Morgan

Mr. Morgan understood a basic tenant of lending – if a borrower doesn't plan to repay a loan, or doesn't care, it is not too hard to hide or falsify information about "money" (future cash flow) or "property" (collateral). More importantly, if assumptions about cash flow and collateral turn out to be incorrect, repayment of an obligation will depend upon the willingness of the obligor to figure out a way to repay. Mr. Morgan believed that the first stop in the extension of credit is to make a judgment about the character of the borrower – the assessment of an obligor's intent and willingness to ensure that the obligation will be repaid, and on time.

Mr. Morgan also referred to "money" and "property". The former (money) refers to the simple fact that obligations are repaid with cash! In the process of making a credit decision, an analyst, banker, investor, must assess the degree to which the obligor will be able to generate enough cash to meet the terms of the debt obligations, either from cash flow, or from the sale or liquidation of assets. As we have stated constantly in this course, the role of a credit analyst is to assess the degree of risk (volatility) of an obligor's future cash flow relative to its fixed obligations. The purpose of financial analysis and cash flow analysis and forecasting, is to reach a conclusion about the degree of volatility of the cash flow of an enterprise and the consequent degree of risk that debt obligations will not be able to be met, as scheduled.

Mr. Morgan's concept of "property" means either direct collateral, or a group of assets owned by the obligor that can be liquidated to pay off an obligation. Most loans are made upon an assumption that they will be repaid from the operating cash flow of the borrower. If cash flow is insufficient, a lender would look to the "second way out" – the liquidation of an asset, either from the pool of assets owned by the obligor, or a specifically assigned or pledged asset which serves as collateral for the obligation.

If an obligor does not make an effort to repay a loan if there is a problem with either cash flow or the value of collateral, it is not always an indication of poor "character". It may be a simple case of a banker who did an inadequate analysis of the risks of the future cash flow of the obligor, and/ or made an poor assumptions about the value of collateral. People with "good character" sometimes allow bankers to make them loans that they cannot afford.

When loans default, some borrowers have been known to state that the default "is not my fault". To the contrary, borrowers have stated to bankers "it's your fault – you gave me the money, and you should have known better!".

The credit and mortgage lending crisis of 2007/2008 is a good example of poorly structured loans based on bad assumptions about obligors' ability to repay, very bad assumptions about the value of collateral (homes), and perhaps naïve assumptions about what a borrower would do if the value of his or her home was less than the outstanding debt. It is also a superb example of bankers who "should have known better".

At the height of the frenzy of mortgage lending in the United States, many home mortgage loans were made without any analysis of the ability of the borrower to repay the debt from his or her net cash flow (cash available for servicing the mortgage debt after other basic personal expenses and debt). Some loans were not supported by any documentary evidence of cash flow or earnings. And, loans were often made equal to or greater than the market value of the property – borrowers were able to finance 100% or close to 100% of the purchase price of a home, even though the debt relative to their ability to service it was very, very high. These were called "sub prime" mortgages – the ability of the borrower to service the debt was questionable.

So, why were these loans made? They were made on an assumption that the value of the collateral would rise at historically high rates, and certainly never fall. These were "one way out" loans – the only way for the loans to be repaid was through the rise in the value of the home, which could be sold or refinanced. Moreover, many loans were made with initial terms that were interest only for a period of time (non amortizing), or very low (below market) interest rates for a certain period of time.

With the crash of home values in many parts of the United States, and the resetting of payments after a grace period of very easy payments, a very large number of borrowers not only defaulted because they didn't have the cash flow to service the debt, but they "turned the keys over to the bank". They walked away from the homes because the value of the home was less than the amount of the outstanding mortgage debt.

These types of loans broke every one of Mr. Morgan's basic premises for making loans that would be paid back. The borrowers' "character" in the form of a credit history was often poor or even unknown. In many cases the cash flow to service the mortgage debt was inadequate or unknown. And, the value of the "property" in the form of collateral was close to the amount of the loan, and in some cases less than the amount of the loan. They were structured entirely on the assumption that the value would increase in a relatively short period of time, and the loan would be refinanced, or repaid from a sale of the collateral in case of default.

The problems created by these poorly structured mortgage loans was compounded by the fact that these loans were packaged into pools of many loans and converted into securities sold to investors. They were "securitized". These securities were structured into many pieces based on the concept of "first loss". Investors received different rates of return based upon where they stood relative to losses in the pool of securities. Certain investors would take the first losses that occurred in the portfolio. Other investors wouldn't take a loss until other investors absorbed losses. The least risky pieces of these securities were assumed to have zero probability of loss – the so-called "super senior" piece. It was assumed that there was plenty of room in the other pieces to absorb all possible losses in any given pool of mortgages. This assumption was wrong! This will be addressed further in the section on securitization.

Credit Structure – Creating Terms and Conditions to Reduce Risk

As has been discussed throughout this course, a primary determinant of credit risk is the nature of the capital structure of an enterprise relative to the nature of its operating risks.

A high risk capital structure is one that has a lot of debt obligations relative to the expected or forecasted free cash flow of the enterprise. If the historic free cash flow is relatively stable, and future free cash flow expected to be stable, an enterprise would be described as one with relatively low operating risk or business risk. If cash flow is stable, the amount of debt service relative to free cash flow can be fairly high. The cash flow volatility is low and the risk of not being able to meet debt service requirements would be relatively low.

Companies, or any type of enterprise, with high operating risk, are best financed with lower amounts of debt relative to the expected cash flow. Cash flow volatility is high and the cash flow cushion relative to debt service requirements must therefore be relatively high. The safest form of capital for companies with volatile cash flow is equity, or instruments with equity characteristics.

One of the lessons of modern corporate finance is that the degree of leverage in the capital structure of a company is a function of the nature of the operating risks of that company and its industry. A longstanding principle for success is to not "mix high operating risk with high financial risk". If cash flow volatility is high due to high operating risk, the capital structure must be relatively conservative with a lot of "patient" capital – i.e., equity type instruments. Otherwise the enterprise runs the risk that free cash flow will not be sufficient at some point in time to meet required debt service payments.

The recent history of financing LEVERAGED BUY OUTS shows that the deals that work in the long run are those where operating risk is relatively low (supermarkets), or where there is a logical and well executed plan for quickly reducing leverage through the sale of assets, or through substantial increases in free cash flow via major cost reductions that are sustainable (i.e., don't destroy the business).

Credit structure, terms, conditions, and covenants are the means via which a company's operating plan and performance is monitored, and to a degree, controlled by creditors. While competition among lenders has reduced the number and nature of terms and conditions in lending agreements, the goals of creating a contract for performance between a lender and a borrower still make sense and are a prudent means of reducing the risks associated with providing financing.

A loan agreement is a contract between a borrower and a lender. For a bond, it's usually in the form of an "indenture". For a private financing, it's simply referred to as a "loan agreement".

Basic terms and conditions in a loan agreement or indenture include:
- repayment schedule
- representations and warranties
- covenants – a set of benchmarks that will be followed or maintained
- events of default

All of the terms and conditions are designed to establish an agreement between the obligor and the creditor (or a group of creditors) about assumptions about the state of the business at the time of the extension of credit, and expectations for performance and repayment during the term of the extension of credit. A credit agreement can cover the extension of credit in different forms, including loans, letters of credit, or derivative contracts.

A breach of terms can lead to a default, which has a variety of remedies which would be incorporated into the agreement via negotiation. The goal of the obligor is to avoid defaults. The goal of the creditor is to be able to cause the obligor to change a situation that led to a default in order to preserve the value of the obligation. In the ultimate case, a default might lead to a demand for full repayment of the obligation, which may or may not be possible. In any event, once a default occurs, or an event that could lead to a default, a dialogue is established between the obligor and creditors to negotiate a solution to the problem that caused a breach in the terms of the agreement, or a potential breach in the terms.

Repayment schedule - At the very least, there is a firm expectation that an obligor will make interest and principal payments as scheduled.

Representations and warranties - These are statements by the obligor that the facts at the time credit is actually extended (the "closing" of the transaction) continue to be true as they were at the time of the signing of the agreement.

Covenants - The extension of credit is based upon analysis about an obligor's ability to fulfill the terms of an obligation. As described in previous lessons, this analysis will provide a forecast of future cash flow from operations and a forecast of uses of that free cash flow for investments, dividends, and debt repayment.

Public debt indentures for investment grade companies (debt rating greater than BBB- by Moody's or Baa3 by S&P) generally do not have covenants, nor any required repayment prior to final maturity.

But term loans extended by banks and private investors usually have financial covenants that, with wide margin for error, establish operating performance and balance sheet parameters that are consistent with the obligor's business plan. They will often also contain some non financial covenants that are designed to prevent a substantial change in the nature of the business or management that was not contemplated at the time of the extension of credit. The number and type of covenants are usually a function of the degree of leverage and financial risk that is perceived to exist with the particular obligation or obligor.

Financial covenants are established within the context of the expectations of the obligor and creditors regarding expected performance, cash flow, and the capital structure. Common financial covenants are:

> Interest coverage - Particularly for highly leveraged situations, a basic covenant is one that monitors interest coverage. It often is in the form of period interest payments (quarterly or annually) relative to cash flow before interest – EBITDA. Earnings before interest, taxes, depreciation and amortization. A variation on this would be a covenant that monitors total debt service to EBITDA; i.e. interest and principal payments.

> Leverage – this might be in the form of a ratio of long term debt to equity, or one of a number of variations, such as equity as a proportion of total tangible assets. The creditors and obligor might also agree to a cap on the amount of debt that can be outstanding.

> Minimum equity – this type of covenant is designed such that a major loss would trigger a default if the absolute amount of equity fell (as a result of the loss, or string of losses) below a certain amount.

> Liquidity – while not used very often, a minimum current ratio (ration of current assets to current liabilities) might be negotiated to enable the creditor to call a default if liquidity falls below a predetermined level.

Non-financial covenants are also established to try to ensure the integrity of the business model upon which credit is extended. These might include:

Change in management

Change in control

Limitation on acquisitions

Limitation on capital expenditures

All covenants are designed to preserve for the creditor, as much as possible, the conditions upon which credit has been extended. They are based upon a business plan and financial forecast that is consistent with the generation of sufficient cash flow to repay the obligation, and within a framework of the risks associated with that forecast of future cash flow.

The structure of an obligation and the terms of a credit agreement are designed to minimize the risk of repayment to the creditor. If forecasted cash flow is large relative to all obligations, the risk is very small, and the terms and conditions are usually minimal. Of course, the analyst or creditor must make an assessment about the risk associated with the future cash flow! If the expected volatility of the future cash flow is low, risk is low. If volatility is high, then the risk is raised.

What are the options available to creditors if the perceived risk of the ability to service an obligation is very high? There are many, most of which employ the assignment of collateral to provide a means of repayment if cash flow proves to be inadequate.

Obligor Risk and Facility Risk – Extending low risk credit to a high risk obligor

Assessing the degree of risk of the future cash flow of an enterprise is the first task of a credit analyst and financial analyst. The financial analyst will use the forecast of "free cash flow" to establish the value of the enterprise. The credit analyst will compare the future cash flow from operations to debt service and try to assess the risk of default of the obligor's debt obligations. This assessment will depend on two factors – the amount of debt relative to cash flow (leverage), and the volatility of the future cash flow.

Credit analysis is the process of making a cash flow forecast, assessing the volatility (or risk) around that forecast, assessing the capital structure and and reaching a judgment about the risk of default in the form of a probability of default. For a rating agency, this will translate into a debt rating. For a bank, it will translate into an obligor risk rating.

A revolution in banking risk management took place in the 1990's – it was credit portfolio management, using obligor risk ratings as its foundation. Banks, and regulators, began to understand that one of the primary reasons for bank failures was concentrations of risk – concentrations by size, obligor, industry, geography, and riskiness. Banks began to manage their risk portfolios to avoid concentrations of risk. They would place limits on how much exposure could be taken to a particular obligor, geography, country, industry. The determining factor was a risk rating. The lower the risk, the more exposure. The higher the risk, the less exposure.

Therefore, identifying the relative and absolute risk of an obligor became a critical part of the process. This was done by establishing and implementing obligor risk ratings.

This process has been incorporated into global bank regulations, in the form of Basel II. Portfolio management, Basel II, and risk ratings, are the subject of the next lesson.

Commercial Finance – Asset Based Extension of Credit

What does a banker, investor, or counter-party do if they receive a request for the extension of credit to an obligor where they think there is a high risk of default? Where, after appropriate analysis, he or she believes that there is a high risk that the obligor will not have the cash to fulfill its obligations in a timely manner.

One option is to not extend credit at all. Another option is to extend credit, but purchase credit default insurance or purchase a credit default swap from another party that is willing to take the risk, for a price! This is an expensive option that may destroy the economic benefit of the investment or extension of credit.

There is another option, which is commonly used, and very effective for the reduction of the risk of loss with an obligor that has a high degree of cash flow risk. It's the assignment of collateral. Through the assignment of collateral to support the extension of credit, and assuming that the collateral has true and sustainable value, it is possible to have a high risk "obligor" but a very low risk credit "facility".

There is an entire aspect of corporate finance that is devoted to the extension of credit to high risk obligors. It is often referred to as "structured finance" or "commercial finance". It uses collateral to substantially reduce the risk of repayment of an obligation, even where the obligor might have a high risk of default. **The objective of structured finance is to create a low risk obligation from a high risk obligor!**

Structured finance is also used to create a presumably low risk obligation from an obligor which may or may not be high risk, but where there is not sufficient information to make a determination. While Mr. Morgan believed that "character" is more important than "money" or "property", it is possible to ignore character if the assigned property is readily valued. Of course, there is always the risk that an unknown, or bad, obligor "character" will provide fraudulent collateral that has little value. There are numerous infamous situations in banking history where this has occurred. (See http://en.wikipedia.org/wiki/Salad_oil_scandal The Wikipedia description of the American Express salad oil swindle in 1963)

A centuries (timeless) means of creating a low risk obligation from a high risk obligor (or one of unknown risk) is to obtain collateral of a known and reliable value, and extending credit at some percentage of that value. If the collateral value is stable and liquid (such as cash!), the advance rate will be high. The greater the risk with the value and liquidity of the collateral, the lower the advance rate.

A well structured commercial finance loan can identify and minimize most of the risks of repayment such that these loans are often "one way out". The primary source of repayment is the liquidation of the collateral. A well structured loan will have collateral of known value and liquidity, along with a significant discount from the estimated value to provide for volatility in the value. The loan amount will usually be made at a substantial discount to the perceived or estimated market value. In this way, a safe loan (or other type of credit extension) can be made to an obligor whose capital structure is weak and where there is a high risk of default on a payment.

The amount extended relative to the value of the collateral is a function of the ability to estimate the future value of the collateral. This is very analogous to forecasting future cash flow – one must understand volatility. In the case of collateral, one must understand the market for reselling the collateral if necessary, and the risk associated with the future value. And, as noted above, a banker must be assured that the obligor is not attempting to commit fraud via "evaporating" collateral.

The types of collateral that are commonly used to secure credit to high risk obligors are: equipment, cash or marketable securities, accounts receivable, inventory and, sometimes, real estate. The highest "advance rates" against collateral are for collateral that is liquid and easy to value. Obviously, cash would be the best, followed by liquid marketable securities, then accounts receivable, inventory, and equipment. Real estate falls across the spectrum. Raw land is illiquid and hard to value. An office building with a long term master lease to a highly rated corporation is much easier to value, and has many of the characteristics of a security. It has stable and predictable cash flow with minor credit risk.

The Commercial Finance industry developed as a means for potential debtors to obtain financing when they could not convince creditors that they had the ability to repay obligations from future cash flow. This industry provides financing based upon the future resale value of pledged collateral of many sorts. In the 20th century, most commercial finance facilities were based upon the direct assignment of equipment, real estate, accounts receivable, and inventory. Accounts receivable collateral is often very closely controlled, with payments to an account or post office box controlled by the creditor.

In the 1980's in the United States, an innovative form of lending was developed to provide financing to companies that were already bankrupt – Debtor in Possession (DIP) financing. The bankruptcy court gave special and preferential protection to lenders who would provide financing, usually against self liquidating assets such as receivables and inventory. Like most "innovative" financing techniques, this actually was a practice of skilled "asset based lenders" long before it became popularized as "DIP" financing. It is a form of very low risk credit extension to creditors with no credit standing!

Equipment financing is widely employed in many industries, but almost none as extensively as in the airline industry. Very few airline companies produce much free cash flow. Yet, even start up or poorly performing airlines are able to obtain financing for aircraft. Specialized finance companies, which have superb skill at estimating future values of various types of aircraft, provide loans or leases to finance most airline fleets around the world. And, losses are relatively small.

On the other hand, equipment finance companies without specialized and extensive knowledge of the market for the sale of used equipment have lost a lot of money! In the case of American Express and the salad oil fraud, there was a presumption that the bankers at Amex were very experienced and sophisticated. This was a situation where Mr. Morgan's advice would have been well taken – the critical aspect of that deal was not "property" it was the "character" of the obligor, which turned out to be people affiliated with organized crime.

Financial Institutions – Margin Credit

Financial institutions and financial investors (including hedge funds) trade huge amounts of securities on a daily basis. Many of these trades, such as derivatives, have relatively long tenors.

The provision of collateral to secure financial transactions is the basis for trillions of dollars of transactions between financial institutions and financial investors. Making a judgment about the "character" of a counter-party is a critical aspect of providing credit for the purchase of securities and the acquisition of risk via derivatives, and is the basis for laws regarding "money laundering" and the principle of "KYC – Know your customer".

But, many investors and funds are private, have limited transparency, and trade in very large volumes relative to their capital. In many situations it is impossible or economically not feasible to try to analyze the credit risk of the counter-parties for these trades. Consequently, for speed and risk management, many if not most of these trades are based primarily on the value of collateral provided to secure the obligation. In the trading world this collateral is referred to as "margin".

During the growth of bank lending to hedge funds in the past 10 years, managers were very concerned about the risks associated with hedge funds, and the difficulty, if not impossibility, of analyzing them. Losses arising from loans to hedge funds have been relatively small, as most of the trades have been secured by marketable and liquid securities, with well established and identifiable value.

Thus, as with commercial finance, assessing character is critical to minimize the risk of loss due to fraud. But understanding how to value collateral, and asses its marketability and liquidity is also critical. While banks have not lost much lending to hedge funds due to rigorous risk standards, they did not seem to apply such rigorous standards to the assessment of collateral in the form of pools of residential mortgages and the investments they made in CDO's (collateralized debt obligations). This will be addressed in the next section on securitization.

In addition to fraud risk and collateral risk, banks dealing in securities trading have another immense risk – operational risk. This is the risk that systems will not be adequate to track outstanding obligations relative to the value of the collateral, or vice versa – to track collateral values relative to the outstanding obligation. This is critical, particularly in rapidly changing markets, to ensure that margin is "called" or liquidated before losses are incurred. Operational risk also applies to the rigorous record keeping that is required in commercial finance account receivable and inventory financing.

Securitization and Special Purpose Vehicles (SPV's)

Securitization is another means by which credit risk is modified and unknown specific risks managed, through the use of the assignment of collateral to ensure the repayment of an obligation. The primary benefit of securitization is that it provides a means of giving non-bank investors the ability to invest in loans that have traditionally been funded only by banks.

It has also permitted the commercial banking system, especially in the United States, to move from an "originate and hold" business model to one of "originate and distribute". Banks now originate loans and sell them to other banks, or package loans, consumer and corporate, into pools which are "securitized" and sold to investors. This transition in the banking business model, from holding risk to distributing it, was strongly encouraged by global banking regulators. But some observers of the credit crisis have attributed this shift to a diminished degree of oversight by banks in terms of analyzing basic risk factors in the loans that they originate for distribution.

The word "securitization" means just what it implies – it is the creation of a security backed by a variety of assets or loans and which is funded by the cash flow exclusively from those assets or loans. The credit crisis that began in 2007 arose in large part due to unexpectedly large default rates on pools of U.S. residential mortgage loans that had been packaged and sold to a variety of individual and institutional investors.

The advantage of securitization to the financial institutions that originate the loans is that the eventual purchasers of the securities do not have recourse for repayment to anything but the cash flow from the amortization of the loans backing the securities. These transactions are "non-recourse" to the originators of the pool of assets or loans.

The non-recourse situation is created by creating a Special Purpose Vehicle (SPV), which in legal terms is "bankruptcy remote". A legal entity is created for the purpose of purchasing a very large number of loans which have been assembled by a bank or other type of financial intermediary. This entity only has one purpose – to purchase the loans with funds from the sale of securities, and to make payments to the owners of the securities from the proceeds of the payments of principal and interest from the loans. Consequently, this entity is known as a Special Purpose Vehicle (SPV) or Special Purpose Entity (SPE). It is "bankruptcy remote" in the sense that no external event can cause it's bankruptcy – it has no creditors other than the investors who purchased the securities is has issued. And, the securities are collateralized by the assets (loans) of the SPV or SPE.

As is constantly outlined in the press in 2008, residential mortgages are a major asset class that has been securitized. But many different types of loans and assets are pooled and sold to SPV's which finance them through the sale of securities. These include credit card loans, automobile loans and leases, student loans, commercial loans and regular corporate trade receivables.

Regardless of the asset class, the technique is similar. A "sponsor" financial institution creates an SPV, and assembles millions of dollars (or other currency) of a certain type of loan or asset to be sold to the SPV, and financed by the sale of securities by the SPV. The key element of the transaction, and the source of the problems of the credit crisis, is that there are minimum credit risk standards that must be met in order for a loan to be accepted into any particular pool.

The pool of loans are collateral for the securities that are issued to fund the purchase of the loans. There are specific criteria established for the risk characteristics of the loans. As with any transaction where the primary "way out" is the liquidation or sale of the collateral, the proportion of assets financed is a function of the risk characteristics of those assets. If the risks are perceived to be low, the advance rate will be high – i.e., the proportion of the total size of the portfolio that will be financed by the securities sold will be high. The remaining amount of the funding for the portfolio, the so-called "equity" piece, will usually be funded by the originator of the loans, which is also often the sponsor of the securitization deal and the SPV.

In "sub-prime" mortgage portfolios, the originators of the securitizations estimated that there would be defaults and losses on some of the mortgages in the securitization pools. The "sub-prime crisis" occurred because losses turned out to be much higher than anticipated, and some investors in these pools incurred losses that were never expected. In other words, losses were greater than the "equity" in the pools.

As is the case with basic commercial finance, the extension of credit that is based upon assumptions about the value of collateral, depends upon a clear understanding of the nature and value of that collateral. If the collateral is a pool of loans, then investors must have a very clear understanding of the underwriting criteria and due diligence of the underlying loans (the collateral). This clearly was not the case for billions of dollars of investments in securitization pools of sub-prime home mortgages. Investors, and in some cases, the bank originators, did not understand the true risk characteristics of some, or many, of the mortgage loans. Or they chose to ignore the risks and assume that the value of the homes secured by the mortgages would continue to rise. The crisis became severe when the value of the collateral behind the mortgages declined, and the individual defaulted because they could not afford to be able to continue to make their mortgage payments.

The lesson of the credit crisis is one of poor underwriting, not one of financial innovation that has gone awry. Securitization is part of the modern world of banking, and will continue. But the awareness of the standards for underwriting the assets in securitization pools must be greater than it has been.

Basic risk analysis is still, and always will be, at the heart of extending credit. This applies to whomever ends up holding the risk of the credit – banks or investors. And, the goal of basic credit analysis is to understand and assess the risk that an obligor will or will not repay an obligation when it is due and in accordance with its terms. In the sub prime mortgage fiasco, investors, banks, and even rating agencies, severely underestimated the basic risks that were inherent in the mortgages that were securitized.

Project Finance

Project finance is another form of structured finance where the collateral for a loan is the assignment of cash flow from a specific enterprise, and where there is little or no recourse to any source of repayment other than the cash flow and assets of that enterprise.

On the surface, this sounds a lot like making an unsecured commercial loan to a business without any outside support! And, that's exactly what it is, with the major exception that in project finance, the vast majority of the cash flow produced by the enterprise is dedicated to the repayment of the debt used to finance the enterprise, and that leverage is usually very high. The collateral to the lender or investor is the entire enterprise; all of its assets and all of its cash flow.

Project finance applies to situations where a "sponsor", a company or government, wishes to use debt for the primary source of funding for a specific project. Repayment of the debt is based primarily upon the cash flow produced by that project, and with little or no recourse for debt repayment to the sponsor.

Funding any enterprise with much more debt than equity works in the long run only if one condition exists – the volatility of future cash flow for the repayment of that debt is very low. In other words, there is very little risk of default. Otherwise, more equity will be required for funding. Providers of debt do not receive a return on investment that is high enough to justify taking high risk. That's the role of equity.

However, there are many types of major projects around the world that can be financed primarily with debt, and where the cash flow to repay that debt is highly predictable and low risk. The traditional use of project finance was in natural resource and transportation projects. The development of large mines or chemical manufacturing facilities has often been financed on a stand alone basis (i.e., project finance) based on the existence of contracts for the sale of the output of the facility. To minimize the risk of the cash flow, these contracts for the purchase of the out were from very large and credit worthy companies, which were also usually the sponsor of the project. The contracts would allow for a purchase price that always covered the cost of the project.

The global shipping industry financed larger oil tankers and bulk carriers using a form of project finance. Independent ship owners would obtain contracts from large oil or commodity companies for the use of the ship that would cover all of the expenses, including debt service. Loans to finance the ships were made to special purpose entities set up to own a single ship, and repayment was entirely from the cash flow produced by that ship, without recourse to the ship owner.

Commercial real estate financing is also a form of project finance. As is the case with large ships, a real estate developer will often build a large office building with a long term lease in place with a major, credit worthy, tenant. The building is owned by a special purpose entity whose only asset is the building. The long term lease payments are sufficient to cover operating expenses and all debt service. The lenders are looking to the primary risk of the tenant, not the real estate developer.

There are also many projects where investors were convinced that the future cash flow would be adequate to service the debt, but where they were greatly mistaken. Euro-Tunnel is one of the prime examples of this. There have also been a number of new toll roads built using project finance, but where the assumptions about cash flow generation turned out to be significantly overestimated. On the other hand, the Australian investment bank, Macquerie, has built a very large business of using project finance and securitization to financing existing infrastructure facilities. It specializes in purchasing facilities, often from local and regional governments, and reselling them to investors. These facilities have a long history of performance, which significantly reduces the risk of predicting future cash flow. Existing airport terminals and toll roads have relatively predictable cash flow, based upon historic operations, and have been purchased and sold with excellent results.

Credit Analysis, Risk and Risk Mitigation

The purpose of credit analysis is to make a judgment about the risk associated with an obligor's ability and willingness to repay an obligation! That means making a judgment about cash flow, as well as the inherent value of the assets of an obligor relative to its obligations.

All extensions of credit are based upon an understanding that cash will exist to repay the obligation. But, cash can come from two sources – cash flow from operations, or the liquidation of an asset. When the creditor believes that the risk of repayment from cash flow is too high relative to the anticipated return, the assignment of collateral can often be used to make the risk / reward equation acceptable. And, there are many cases where credit can be extended solely on the value of the collateral. But just as the lender against cash flow must understand all of the factors than impact future cash flow, the lender against an asset must fully understand the factors that will affect the value and marketability of that asset.

Chapter 9

Managing Credit Risk - Risk Ratings and Portfolio Management

Managing Credit Risk and the Credit Crisis of 2008

What were the fundamental causes of the 2008 Credit Crisis? In the spring of 2008, a U.S. radio program explored the issue with the question:

"Why are they lending money to people who can't afford to pay it back."? (National Public Radio – "This American Life")

The purpose of credit analysis is to identify the degree of risk that an obligor will or will not be able to fulfill a credit obligation. Providers of credit expect to be repaid in full, and on time, and with a return on investment that is appropriate for the risk assumed. This applies to all forms of credit extension – loans, derivative contracts, letters of credit, trade credit, and investments in debt instruments.

Identifying the "degree of risk" in a credit obligation is critical to modern risk management and risk investing for a number of reasons:

- The expected return on investment or the price to be charged should be higher or lower, depending upon the risk of repayment

- Credit risk portfolio management is now a fundamental part of risk management, for both investors and providers of credit. Identifying an appropriate risk rating or credit rating for all obligations or investments is an integral part of portfolio management, as risks are distributed within a portfolio in accordance with risk ratings.

- New rules for determining minimum levels of bank capital are based upon obligor and obligation risk ratings.

In the events leading up to the 2008 Credit Crisis, a very large number of financial institutions, rating agencies, and investors did not have an adequate understanding of the fundamental credit risks that were imbedded in residential mortgage backed securities. Many of these residential loans only had "one way out" – the sale or refinancing of the residence based upon steadily increasing market values. Repayment by cash flow was often not a consideration.

Moreover, many investors believed that they were protected against the risk of default by virtue of the existence of other investors who were subordinate in the pools of securities, and who would take losses before them. These pools of securities were divided into "tranches", each with different risks of loss, ranging from high (rated less than BBB) to very low (rated AA or AAA). However, the underlying mortgages each had a relatively high risk of default – they were made with very lax underwriting standards.

As the US and European economies deteriorated in 2009, and as liquidity became scarce, we saw that many banks and investors ignored the cash flow risks associated with making loans to highly leveraged companies, regardless of the operating risks of their industry.

Early in this course we stated that companies go bankrupt for one of three reasons:
- they run out of cash
- they fear that they will run out of cash, or
- their suppliers of liquidity fear that they will run out of cash

This is basically what happened to Lehmann, Bear Stearns, Merrill, and AIG. Anticipated losses in obligations related to sub prime loans, and securitizations of sub prime loans, were greater than the capital of the companies. They tried (and succeeded to a degree) to raise new capital, but the "marked to market" losses in a variety of esoteric securities caused the providers of credit to these companies to withhold new extensions of credit.

In the summer and autumn of 2008, the suppliers of liquidity (in the form of short term credit facilities) to some investment banks stopped. In the case of AIG, the US Federal Reserve Bank of NY provided an $85 billion credit facility in order to allow for an orderly liquidation of the company.

All of this stress was due to fundamental credit risk! The investment banks were underwriters of huge amounts of asset backed securities known, amongst other names, as CDO's – collateralized debt obligations. These were publicly issued bonds that were secured (collateralized) by groups of individual loans, which were in turn secured by residential mortgages. The problem stemmed from the fact that the underlying individual loans (home mortgage loans), were made with very weak, and perhaps, non-existent, credit criteria. Most of the loans were originated based on credit criteria that had only "one way out". In many cases, the income of the borrower was not sufficient to service the loans over time. Many were structured with low monthly payments in the early years, with rapidly escalating payments later on.

The demise of Lehmann and Bear Stearns has shown that these firms were much more highly leveraged than was appreciated or understood by investors. When concern arose about the quality (and liquidity) of the assets supporting this leverage, suppliers of liquidity took their money and ran for safety. This is very similar to what happened to Enron in 2002. Suppliers of liquidity fled when they realized that Enron was really a highly leveraged financial trading company, not a moderately leveraged pipeline company.

Credit risk, and the ignorance of some major credit risk issues, was the core reason behind the 2008 credit crisis. It may have been the "necessary" condition for the crisis, but it wasn't the "sufficient" condition. **The crisis was caused by bad credit risk judgment and bad credit risk management, along with a weak regulatory environment.**

The crowning blow to the institutions that suffered substantial losses was huge concentrations of these assets relative to their earnings and capital. A very common theme in news reports about the crisis was about financial institutions in need of additional capital to maintain leverage within a normal, but stretched, standard due to the losses in the sub prime investments.

Modern credit risk management, like modern portfolio investment management, is based upon the diversification of risk and the avoidance of "concentrations". Financial institutions and investors in credit risk are supposed to be managed in a way that minimizes the risk that problems in one asset class can cause unusually large losses. In the 2008 crisis, the rules of portfolio management and the avoidance of risk concentrations seems to have been ignored, at least until it was too late or almost too late.

The regulation of the global banking system by various central banks is, first and foremost, designed to minimize global financial systemic risk. The work of the Basel Committee on Banking Supervision, in conjunction with the world's central banks, is designed to ensure that credit crises don't occur. They began to institute suggestions for credit risk portfolio management in the 1990's.

Modern credit risk management is based upon credit risk portfolio management. It is designed to ensure that various types of risk are well distributed within an institution or investor, without undo concentrations. **Credit analysis, and the creation of obligor risk ratings, is at the heart of credit risk portfolio management**. It is impossible to pursue credit risk portfolio management without a rigorous system of establishing risk ratings for each obligation in a portfolio. The quantification of a judgment about the risk of a creditor or an obligation is evidenced by a risk rating or a debt rating.

Despite very strong efforts on the part of bank regulators to impose credit risk portfolio management on their constituent banks, the Credit Crisis of 2008 did occur! This was not entirely due to lack of oversight by the Central Bankers of the world. Other major factors behind this crisis are related to financial market developments that were thought by many to actually reduce banking industry systemic risk.

- Credit risk has become a "traded product". Modern techniques of corporate finance, securitization and derivatives, have allowed banks to "distribute" credit risk to investors. This is a critical component of active credit risk portfolio management.

- The traditional "originate and hold" model of commercial banking has been transformed into a model of "originate and distribute". This change has been broadly encouraged by bank regulators as a means of reducing risk to the banking system. Credit risk has been structured by banks so that it can be sold to new classes of investors for credit risk – institutional investors such as pension funds, mutual funds, hedge funds, and insurance companies.

- A "shadow" banking system has evolved due to the development of securitization which has allowed originators of credit risk to bypass banks entirely, and sell loans to investment banks, which package them into securities to be sold to investors.

The ability to distribute credit risk was primarily due to:

- the creation and use of risk ratings,
- proprietary risk rating models that predicted rates of default based upon published ratings,
- the growth of credit "asset classes" that made it possible for investors to purchase credit risk directly from the originators, often without passing through a bank. The credit risk decision was made by investors, rather than bankers, often using rating agencies as a proxy for the credit decision.

An apparent result of the distribution of credit risk away from commercial banks has been a tendency to ignore, or make opaque, the underlying nature of the risks being acquired. In the case of US "sub-prime" mortgages, investors may not have realized the actual nature of the risk that they were acquiring. They may have relied too heavily upon the analysis or assurances of rating agencies and the bankers who originated, packaged, and sold the risk in the form of securities – CDO's or CMO's. Some analysts and commentators suggest that the originators and distributors of these loans were more focused on generating fees than on the quality of the credit that was being originated.

The actual defaults in many portfolios of sub prime mortgages turned out to be significantly higher than forecasted. Many of the investments were structured to avoid any loss – portfolios were divided and sold according to the degree to which an investor would be subject to actual defaults. Defaults affected investors whose expectation of any loss was next to zero.

The huge growth in these low quality mortgage loans was due, in large part, to the growth of the "shadow" banking system. The rapid growth of "securitization" provided a mechanism whereby these individual mortgage loans could be originated and placed outside of the traditional banking system. Loans were originated by mortgage "brokers" who sold them to investment banks. The investment bank would "warehouse" the loans, hold them on their books, until there were enough that they could assemble into a package, created a security backed by these loans, the "CDO", and sell the CDO securities to investors. The traditional risk management practices of banks seems to have been bypassed by the brokers who were paid well to originate loans, and by the investment banks who had tremendous demand from investors due to the higher relative yield on the bonds that presumably carried very little risk.

The issue was succinctly summarized in a September 2008 note by a reporter from Bloomberg News....

> "Flawed AAA ratings on mortgage-backed securities that turned to junk now lie at the root of the world financial system's biggest crisis since the Great Depression, according to more than 50 former ratings professionals, investment bankers, academics and consultants.
>
> ``I view the ratings agencies as one of the key culprits," says Joseph Stiglitz, 65, the Nobel laureate economist at Columbia University in New York. ``They were the party that performed that alchemy that converted the securities from F-rated to A-rated. The banks could not have done what they did without the complicity of the ratings agencies."

Driven by competition for fees and market share, the New York-based rating agency companies stamped out top ratings on debt pools that included $3.2 trillion of loans to homebuyers with bad credit and undocumented incomes between 2002 and 2007. As subprime borrowers defaulted, the companies have downgraded more than three-quarters of the structured investment pools known as collateralized debt obligations issued in the last two years and rated AAA.

Without those AAA ratings, the gold standard for debt, banks, insurance companies and pension funds wouldn't have bought the products. Bank writedowns and losses on the investments totaling $523.3 billion led to the collapse or disappearance of Bear Stearns Cos., Lehman Brothers Holdings Inc. and Merrill Lynch & Co. and compelled the Bush administration to propose buying $700 billion of bad debt from distressed financial institutions.

``The part that became the most aggravating -- personally irritating -- is that CDO guys everywhere didn't want to know fundamental credit analysis; they didn't want to know from being in touch with the underlying asset," says a Moody's analyst who quit in January 2001 after being reassigned out of the residential mortgage-backed securities business.
``There is no substitute for fundamental credit analysis."

The bankers and rating agencies used proprietary "models" and assumptions that estimated that losses from these mortgage portfolios would occur within historic norms. They apparently didn't realize (or didn't care) that these were "one way out" loans. Since cash flow from the obligors was either insufficient to service the mortgage loans, or there was insufficient information to determine if the future cash flow to service the loans was adequate, the loans were made on an assumption that the value of the properties would be sufficient to repay the loans in case of default, or at least to minimize losses.

In many of the securitizations of these loans, it was assumed that there was only a very small probability that losses would exceed 10% - 15% of the face value of the loans. In retrospect, the ultimate losses are unknown, but many portfolios experienced defaults will in excess of this range. This is why the securities with "AAA" ratings have been drastically impaired. Owners of these securities were at risk only if default rates exceeded a certain amount, probably in the range of 10% of the face value of the portfolio. Defaults have been much higher than that.

Managing Credit Risk – Portfolio Management and Risk Ratings

The identification of the risk of repayment is the fundamental goal of credit analysis. This applies to analysis for investors in credit instruments (notes and bonds), rating agencies, lenders (banks or finance companies), suppliers of merchandise (trade creditors), counterparties (derivatives) or indirect suppliers of credit (guarantors or issuers of letters of credit).

The process of risk assessment includes:

- o financial analysis to assess historical operating and performance, cash flow generation, and capital structure
- o industry analysis to understand operating and competitive risks, and industry key success factors
- o capital structure adequacy relative to operating and business risks and existing financial risk,
- o business strategy and management assessment,
- o cash flow forecasting to determine free cash flow and debt capacity, and
- o judgment about character.

The job of a credit analyst is to quantify the relative degree of risk associated with an obligation. For bank analysts this usually is done in the form of a risk rating. For a rating agency, it's the debt rating. In either case, the job is to create an assessment of an obligation that is analogous to the probability of default.

Rating agencies have formalized this with statistical models that try to correlate a specific rating to an actual probability of default. Large, complex, global banks have established models that are similar to those of rating agencies.

For the manager of a portfolio of a number of credit obligations, risk needs to be managed to ensure that the portfolio is well balanced across the risk spectrum, and without undue concentrations. The portfolio manager has the capability to modify the nature of its credit risk investment portfolio through a number of risk management tools, which include trading of assets, securitization of credit risk assets, and the purchase of insurance against some of the risk.

The quantification of risk assessment, via the establishment of a risk rating or debt rating, is critical for modern credit risk management. We no longer live in a world where it is sufficient to make a risk decision with a "yes" or a "no". An effective system for establishing and using ratings has three key benefits:

-   it facilitates portfolio management – an institution's portfolio can be balanced by credit risk ratings, as well as other risk factors such as industry and geography.

-   it provides a basis for establishing the right "price" for the extension of credit – the required return on capital for the investment in a credit product should be adjusted for the degree of risk

-   it provides the basis for a discussion about the merits of the extension of credit that are distinct from the tension created by the demand for a "yes" or "no" decision. This tension can be extreme between originators of risk transactions (bankers or investors) and risk managers. The tension is better managed when the discussion is centered upon the relative degree of risk and the return that is to be achieved.

Once the degree of risk of an obligor and specific obligation has been established, the risk of repayment can be addressed and managed via the structure of credit facilities, including the use of collateral, the sale of different risk assets, or the use of credit derivatives (credit default swaps) to "lay off" some of the risk.

The Practice of Managing Credit Risk – Trade Credit and Supplier Financing

The primary goal of a supplier of trade credit is to sell merchandise and receive a profit on the sale of that merchandise. The reason to extend credit to a buyer of that merchandise is to facilitate the sale. In some cases, the profit margin may be so high that the seller is willing to take a large risk that the buyer will default. The seller can afford to take a certain degree of credit losses in exchange for a larger sales volume and greater profit.

During the telecom and internet boom of the late 1990's, many manufacturers of equipment provided extended financing terms to financially weak startup companies in order to build volume and profit. Unfortunately, the burst of the internet and telecom "bubble" turned a lot of this "vendor" financing paper into rubble and many manufacturers were destroyed by their inability to collect from there customers. This perhaps was the epitome of naïve or ignorant credit extension and the balancing of "risk" and "reward". These vendors assumed huge risk in anticipation of moderate reward, and the equation failed.

On the other hand, if profit margins are small, a single credit loss can wipe out the profit from a large number of sales. This seller will want to be very conservative in the extension of credit – they can't afford to lose money by taking risk from customers. But, in some industries, competition is such that suppliers must provide a certain degree of short term credit to their customers. A prime example is the relationship between apparel manufacturers and large retailing companies. The power of the retailers is such that vendors have no choice but to provide trade credit for 30 to 90 days. Yet many vendors are small companies and cannot afford any credit loss due to the failure of a major customer.

This is why the "factoring" industry exists. Finance company's, often referred to as "factors", purchase, without recourse, the receivables due to apparel (or other) manufacturers. The price of the purchase is a discount from the face value (the amount due), which reflects two things – the costs of money (the interest rate factor), and the credit risk. The higher the credit risk, the larger the discount.

In the process of "factoring" – the sale of short term accounts receivable to a specialized finance company – credit risk is transferred from a manufacturer to a finance company. The burden of credit analysis is now placed on the finance company. It must decide how much credit risk it is willing to accept from a particular obligor.

Analysts at the finance company will pursue the same process that has been described in this course. They will try to assess the degree of volatility in the future cash flow of the obligor in order to assess the long term credit risk. For short term receivables, they will also address liquidity issues. But they will also adhere to the age old maxim that was described in an earlier lesson of this course – "never lend short where you wouldn't lend long". This is the lesson that if an obligor cannot meet a short term obligation, the creditor now is in for the long term, and will get repaid (hopefully) from future cash flow.

The factoring company (finance company) has another dilemma. Like all good investors, it will practice "portfolio management". It will try to maintain a balance sheet with risk exposure that is well balanced, but it also needs to serve its manufacturing clients who cannot afford to carry the accounts receivable of their retailing industry customers.

The factor's dilemma is one of how to serve its own clients, by buying all of the accounts receivable that they wish to sell, but also by pursuing good credit risk portfolio management by avoiding "concentration risk".

"Concentration risk" is perhaps the single most significant issue in credit risk management – it is the risk of too much exposure, relative to capital, to a single asset class, whether it be one obligor, one industry, one geography, or one country.

Diversification is the goal for survival in any investment portfolio – loans or equities. Excessive concentration (relative to capital) in sub prime mortgage assets (directly or indirectly) was the cause of the 2008 failures of Bear Stearns, Lehmann, and AIG, and the near failure of Merrill Lynch. Too much exposure, relative to capital, of commercial real estate loans was the cause of a number of U.S. banking failures in the early 1990's. It was also the cause of the demise in the UK of Northern Rock in 2007 and Bradford and Bingley in 2008.

So, the managers of the factoring company, or any finance company, or bank, or supplier of credit, or fixed income pension fund investor, mutual fund manager, insurance company portfolio manager, or individual investor, will try to maintain a portfolio of diversified risk, and presumably at investment returns that reflect the degree of risk. **The necessary condition for the creation of a diversified portfolio of risk assets (banks) or fixed income investments (investors), is the ability to establish a risk rating for each obligation.**

Once the acquirer of a risk asset (bank, finance company, investor, etc.) establishes the portfolio risk parameters with which they are comfortable, their goal will be to maintain risk assets in that portfolio in the proportions that are established by their portfolio management policies. If they have a very low tolerance for risk, they will try to maintain a portfolio with less risky exposure, and presumably slightly lower returns. The goal of the managers of the credit risk portfolio is to obtain a return on capital that is appropriate for the risks assumed. Economists, and bank regulators, refer to this as "risk adjusted" return on capital, or "return on economic capital".

This example of a factoring company (finance company), is directly applicable to all entities that extend credit – banks, insurance companies, and direct investors in credit instruments – mutual funds, pension funds, etc.

If the portfolio managers find that they do not have a distribution of credit risk that is consistent with their portfolio goals, what do they do? In other words, if they have too much exposure to a particular obligor, or geography, or industry, how do they manage this?

The simple, and traditional, means of managing this is that they shut down business with that obligor or sector! They will "just say no" when they receive a request for additional exposure, until their existing exposure is reduced to a satisfactory level. Of course, there is always pressure from clients, and the business managers, to "waive" the rules set by portfolio management, and take on more exposure.

The modern, and more complex, means of managing concentration risk and portfolios is the use of credit derivatives or securitization to distribute risk outside of the portfolio. This has the very significant benefit of maintaining client relationships, spreading risk, and providing credit risk investment opportunities to non-traditional investors, or to investors who do not have easy access to the credit risk of certain obligors.

Risk Rating Methodology and Portfolio Management

Credit risk portfolio management cannot exist without a system for quantifying relative credit risk in the form of an obligor's risk rating or debt rating. The method of establishing a risk rating or debt rating is a direct result of the processes described in this course. Analysts must establish the degree of volatility in an obligor's future operating cash flow, and free cash flow, reflecting the nature of fixed obligations and the level of amortizing debt in the capital structure. This is done via an in depth understanding of the obligor's management and strategy, its industry, its competitive position within its industry, and the nature of its capital structure relative to its business risk and volatility.

Rating agencies, which will rate publicly issued (and sometimes privately placed) fixed income securities, have well established frameworks, historic models and statistics in place for determining the risk characteristics of many industries, and analyzing companies within those industries. Their goal is to establish a probability of default, and translate that into a particular debt rating. The process is based upon financial analysis to establish benchmarks of historic performance, and capital structure. These are compared with the historic performance of companies within a similar industry – companies that succeed and companies that fail. However, the qualitative aspect of the rating process is as important, if not more important, than the quantitative. Analysts, and senior rating agency managers, are concerned about the nature of a company's management and its attitude towards risk. The actual rating is the result of a committee process, not a purely statistical model.

Many fixed income investors are guided in the management of their portfolios by these public ratings. Historically, many pension fund and insurance company investors were not permitted to invest at all in "non-investment" grade securities – fixed income obligors or specific securities that were rated less than BBB- (Standard and Poors) or Baa3 (Moody's). One of the lessons of the events of 2007 and 2008 is that investors take a risk if they rely exclusively on public ratings, without any independent analysis.

Banks, trade creditors, and finance companies, often, if not always, deal with companies that do not have public debt ratings. Consequently, they must establish their own mechanisms and models for creating relative risk ratings if they are to manage their portfolios in a diversified manner. Their goals are similar – they need to avoid "concentrations" in a risk class such that if it were to default, it could destroy the company. In general, risk managers and portfolio managers are trying to minimize exposure to obligors where the event of a loss would "eat" through the capital of the company.

Credit Derivatives, Credit Insurance, and Credit Default Swaps

The huge insurance company, AIG, suffered losses due to its ability and willingness to provide a guarantee to investors against their potential loss in the investment in a mortgage backed security. A non-insurance subsidiary of AIG earned fees by guaranteeing portions of CDO portfolios against loss. This is pure credit risk transfer. For a relatively small fee, the owner of a CDO could transfer all or a portion of its portfolio credit risk to another party (in this case, an AIG company). The party accepting the risk would be making its own credit decision about the probability of loss. In the case of CDO's, there seems to have been a significant lack of fundamental credit analysis exercised.

In most instances of guaranteeing against credit loss, the current mechanism used is a Credit Default Swap, which is also known as a Credit Derivative. Credit derivatives effectively transfer credit risk, while allowing the investor to retain the obligation as an asset.

A credit default swap is directly analogous to credit insurance or the issuance of a clean letter of credit. In exchange for a fee, a creditor can buy risk protection from another entity. In other words, this "seller" of protection guarantees that the creditor will not suffer any loss of principle in case the obligor defaults. As in a clean letter of credit, the beneficiary of the protection will be paid a certain amount (usually the full principle amount due) if the obligor either does not pay, or defaults on another obligation. The nature of the default, or trigger event, is defined in the credit protection agreement. In the early days of credit default swaps, the triggering event was often an actual "event of default" as defined in public bond debenture agreements.

Credit derivatives (credit default swaps) have become a major means for creditors and investors to pursue active credit risk portfolio management. Their use has allowed banks and finance companies to continue to provide credit to their clients, even when their exposure is larger than desired. Credit derivatives have allowed them to extend credit, but purchase protection to reduce the net exposure.

The sellers of credit protection are often other financial institutions which are also pursuing credit portfolio management. The use of credit derivatives has had the effect of "globalizing" the distribution of credit risk. In the early days of the development of credit derivatives, some financial institutions used them to INCREASE their exposure to a particular obligor, geography, or industry. Following credit portfolio management, they had "room" to increase particular categories of risk, but did not have the ability to directly participate in a bank loan syndicate, or purchase public securities. So, they entered into credit default swaps with financial institutions that did desire to reduce risk.

The CDS market grew tremendously between 1998 and 2008, sometimes driven by speculation, as well as profit opportunity. It expanded from corporate credit to many different types of credit risk, including residential and commercial real estate mortgages, and the securities made up of pools of those mortgages (CDO's).

One of the key lessons learned from the Credit Crisis, and one that was dismissed by many traders, is that one should not trade any product without fully understanding the inherent risks. If credit risk is being traded, one must understand the underlying credit risk. Otherwise trading becomes a game of "musical chairs". When the music stops, someone is left holding the risk (or is left without a place to sit!). In retrospect, it is clear that many significant participants in the credit markets prior to 2008, did not understand the fundamental risks inherent in instruments that were being underwritten and sold, or which were traded.

Basel II and Bank Portfolio Management and Risk Ratings

As a result of the suggestions of the Basel Committee on Banking Supervision, incorporated in the accords know as "Basel I" (1988) and "Basel II (2004), rigorous credit portfolio management has become a central part of risk management at most large banks, throughout the world. Rigorous risk and capital management requirements are designed to ensure that a bank holds capital appropriate to the risk the bank exposes itself to through its lending and investment practices. The greater risk to which the bank is exposed, the greater the amount of capital the bank needs to hold to safeguard its solvency and overall economic stability. Basel II also incorporates capital requirements for other types of banking risks such as operational risk and market risk.

Portfolio management was initiated by large commercial banks in the 1980's after various credit crises established the fact that banks usually failed due to "concentration risk" – unduly large concentrations of risk, relative to the capital base, in a particular industry or geography.

The globalization of the use of portfolio management by commercial banks was formalized in 1988 with the minimum bank capital proposals of "Basel I" from the Basle Committee and the Bank for International Settlements. The first Basel agreement established suggested rules for basic capital requirements for global commercial banks. While applications varied by country, most Central Banks and bank regulators adopted the basic Basel requirements for their local banks. This was the first step in rudimentary portfolio management for banks. Different levels of capital were required for commercial risk, consumer risk, financial institutions, and governments. It was very crude, as there was no differentiation for corporate risk. Banks had to maintain the same amount of capital for all corporate / commercial obligations, without regard to the nature of the risk of these obligations. Less capital was required for obligations from certain financial institutions and governments.

Basel II was developed in the late 1990's and formally proposed in 2004. The goal was to establish bank minimum capital requirements that were more closely aligned with the actual risk characteristics of a bank's credit portfolio. The higher the perceived risk of an obligation, the more capital would be required. For globally complex and sophisticated banks, capital for credit risk will be allocated according to the distribution of actual credit risk within a portfolio. Consequently, the implementation of Basel II requires the risk rating of each obligation within a portfolio. Basel II also establishes capital requirements for Operational Risk – the risk associated with "unexpected losses", such as those arising from lawsuits. Expected losses, from the loan portfolio, will usually be incorporated into a bank's capital structure via "reserves" for losses. Capital exists to cover "unexpected" losses.

The challenge for implementing credit portfolio management in a bank is the need to place a "risk rating" on every obligation. This required a major change in the nature of credit analysis and assessment in banks.

Traditionally, a credit analyst was asked to say "yes" or "no" to a request for an extension of credit. The emphasis of this course has been that the role of a credit analyst is to assess the degree of risk associated with the repayment of an obligation.
In modern credit risk management, decisions are no longer "yes" or "no". The first step in a credit decision is to assess the degree of risk of repayment. In banks, that's the establishment of a risk rating. The decision process that emanates from this is a function of a creditor's portfolio management policy. It is based upon the establishment of a risk rating, for obligors and for obligations. The use of collateral to reduce the risk of repayment can also change the risk rating of an obligation. Because of "structure", including collateral, it is possible to have a better risk rating on an obligation, than that of the obligor.

Credit Risk Management - Summary

The quantification of a judgment about the risk of a creditor or an obligation is evidenced by a risk rating or a debt rating. Once a risk rating is established, an investor or a creditor can make a decision about assuming that risk. That decision will be a function of the return to be achieved, and the degree to which the risk is acceptable, regardless of the return. The decision about the willingness to accept a degree of risk is a key element in modern credit risk management – portfolio management.

This course has been about how this is done. Credit analysis is about making a judgment about the cash flow volatility of a creditor and how that volatility could impact a creditor's ability to make all necessary payments on its obligations. Credit risk *management* is about how to achieve the goals of a risk portfolio – attaining high returns, meeting client needs, and not assuming concentration risks that can destroy the portfolio's returns, or even the institution.

www.ingramcontent.com/pod-product-compliance
Lightning Source LLC
Chambersburg PA
CBHW070901180526
45168CB00005B/1893